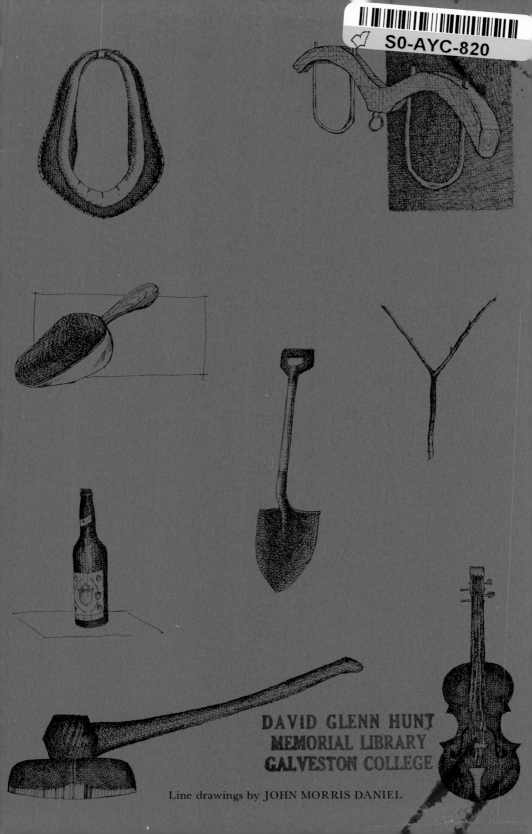

Line drawings by JOHN MORRIS DANIEL

SOME STILL DO:
Essays on Texas Customs

Publications of The Texas Folklore Society Number XXXIX

SOME STILL DO:

Essays on Texas Customs

Edited by

FRANCIS EDWARD ABERNETHY

1975   THE ENCINO PRESS   AUSTIN

To
Ralph W. Steen, President,
Stephen F. Austin State University,
Who is a good friend to the Society.

First Edition
© 1975: Texas Folklore Society: Nacogdoches
Published by The Encino Press: 510 Baylor Street: Austin

AMATEUR AND PROFESSIONAL FOLKLORISTS

By Wilson M. Hudson

W HEN I chose to talk about amateur and professional folklorists, I felt sure that I should not be raising an issue that would split the Society into two factions. Within our ranks these distinguishable kinds of folklorists have existed very happily together, without being uncomfortably aware that there might be differences to fall out about. The last thing I should want to do is to create a division amongst us.

How are amateurs and professionals in folklore to be distinguished from one another? Let us leave out of consideration the question of how one makes one's living, which doesn't go to the heart of the matter. In general an amateur is someone who takes an interest and participates in a certain activity without observing a set of established principles and procedures. The professional, on the other hand, commits himself to the principles and procedures which have gained acceptance as producing the best results in his field of activity. He plays the game by the rules and in the prescribed manner.

Amateurs and professionals often think and sometimes say harsh things about each other. When the amateur is in a critical mood it seems to him that the professional's work is unoriginal, cut-and-dried, and lifeless. For his part the professional may wish that the amateur would not dabble in a field where he has no competence and can only spoil whatever he lays his hand to. When feeling more charitable, the professional can appreciate the amateur's enthusiasm and verve though he must deplore his lack of direction and discipline. And the amateur occasionally has to admit that the professional possesses a

Read on the evening of April 20, 1973, at the dinner of the Texas Folklore Society given in connection with its annual meeting. The speaker, who was made a Fellow of the Society at its previous meeting, served as Associate Editor from 1951 to 1964 and as Secretary-Editor from 1964 to 1971.

range of knowledge and a sureness of purpose which are impressive in spite of his unemotional presentation.

There is one kind of amateur whom the professional can look upon with tolerance and even pride—that is, the forerunner who takes part in defining a new subject matter and in formulating an appropriate method of studying it. Since this man does his work before the rules have been established, he is necessarily an amateur; but since he helps establish the rules, he can be looked upon as preprofessional. That is to say, he is not yet a professional but he is on the road to becoming one. His role is that of a gifted beginner or a revered pioneer.

In the development of all the separate branches of the humanities, new fields have come into existence through the efforts of amateurs whose inclinations and enthusiasms led them to concentrate upon some phase or aspect of human activity, so that in time it could be seen as meriting and demanding special study in a particular manner.

This was the process which gave rise to the large and inclusive field now denominated "folklore studies." To take only one subject forming a part of these studies, let me review how the ballad passed from the stage of amateur interest to the stage of professional study. You will recall that Sir Philip Sidney said that the old song of Percy and Douglas could move his heart more than the blowing of a trumpet, and that Addison devoted a paper in the *Spectator* to "Chevy Chase" as an heroic poem. It was not until 1765 that a considerable collection of popular songs in English was published. Bishop Percy's *Reliques of Ancient English Poetry* is a landmark. The good Bishop loved the songs or he would not have busied himself with them, but he did not feel obliged to print the texts just as they appeared in the MS which had fallen into his hands. Comparison with the versions in his folio MS shows that he made changes for the sake of literary improvement. From the professional's point of view today, this was reprehensible, but Bishop Percy can be forgiven because he gave an impetus to further collection and study simply by printing ballads in a book. Besides, he did leave the original MS versions behind. It can be said that Bishop Percy was preprofessional.

Let us now take a big skip to F. J. Child's five-volume collection of *English and Scottish Popular Ballads* (1882–98). Child was professional in that he undertook to bring together all the known variants of popular ballads and to give information about the dating and provenience of each item. He used numbers as headings so that related variants could be kept together as members of the same basic type. The result is that today the Child numbers provide us with a ready means of classifying ballads. If a newly discovered ballad can't be placed under one of the 305 Child numbers, then another number can be set up for it.

When John A. Lomax was a boy in Bosque County he heard cowboys singing songs as they went about their work. He wrote them down and brought them along when he came to the University of Texas. Morgan Callaway, then head of the English department, discouraged Lomax's pursuit of the ballad as a topic of literary study because it couldn't be connected with any major writer or movement. When Lomax went on to Harvard, however, George Lyman Kittredge, who had been a student of Child's there, encouraged him to continue his interest in the ballad. After his year at Harvard, Lomax returned to Texas A & M College bringing with him Kittredge's suggestion that he should organize a branch of the American Folklore Society to collect folklore in Texas. A conversation in 1909 between Lomax and L. W. Payne, a teacher of English at the University who had a special interest in the dialects of Southern English, resulted in a joint decision to found the Texas Folklore Society.

John A. Lomax's initial love of folksongs never diminished throughout his long and productive life. With his son Alan he edited several collections with full historical and comparative notes, but it is very likely that to him the most important thing remained the immediate experience of the ballad as folk art.

When young Stith Thompson came to Austin to teach at the University in 1914, by good luck he happened to rent a room from John A. Lomax, then back on the campus as registrar. Lomax invited Thompson to join the Society, and in 1916 Thompson edited the first volume of Publications of the Folk-Lore Society of Texas. Stith Thompson did not remain long at the University; he went on to Colorado College in Colorado Springs and eventually to the University of Indiana at Bloomington. He revised Antti Aarne's *Types of the Folktale*, and planned and edited both editions of the monumental *Motif-Index of Folk-Literature*. There can be no doubt that he is the world's leading exponent of the Finnish method of studying folk narratives of all kinds. This method traces the origin and dissemination of a particular narrative by dating all of the variants and locating them geographically. It works comparatively by means of a system of analysis and classification of tale-types and by means of a smaller-scale discrimination of motifs, each with a number assigned for identification. As refined and expanded by Thompson, the Finnish method is in a high degree professional in that its techniques and procedures have been clearly worked out, have gained general acceptance, and have produced very considerable results.

Through the years Thompson has maintained his membership in the Society, though he has not contributed an article to our Publications since the first volume appeared. In the spring of 1956 he was on the campus of the University as a visiting professor and gave a course in the folktale. He and Dobie were good friends from 1916 on. It was Mody Boatright who brought Thompson back to Austin for a visit.

Dobie edited the second volume of our Publications in 1923 and he continued to function as editor down through the volume for 1941. At the start he was imbued with the desire to do for legends and tales what Lomax had done for Texas folksongs. In his later years Dobie said he did not consider himself a folklorist but a storyteller. If a story was interesting he made no further demands upon it. He acknowledged freely that he had a "constructive memory"—that is, after hearing a story he might alter it to make it better. He never thought of himself as simply a transcriber of tales who was bound to reproduce the original exactly as he had heard it, and he never developed a tolerance for tape recorders as a device to aid the collector. He had very pliant ideas about what might be considered folklore. Mody Boatright, who became associate editor in 1937, relates that if a paper submitted for publication did not fit into an accepted category of folklore and Dobie thought it good, he would say, "It doesn't matter. We make our own categories." We should say today that Dobie had an "open" concept of folklore. Such a concept is hardly acceptable to professional folklorists, but it gives the amateur of folkish matters great freedom to pursue a line which leads him on. Dobie, for example, was free to recognize a mixture of folklore and history and to deal with it in a volume of the Society's Publications entitled *In the Shadow of History*.

Dobie was not very friendly to the Finnish method of studying folklore comparatively. He was reluctant to take seriously the theory that the story of B'rer Rabbit and the Tar Baby had a history of migration from India to Africa and on to America. He thought that tale-type numbers and motif numbers were academic paraphernalia.

The long term of Dobie's editorship was a period great in the collecting of all kinds of folklore. He ranged far and wide in the Southwest—including Mexico—and he wrote down much for our Publications and got many others who had never taken particular notice of something as familiar as folklore to send in legends, folktales, ballads, and sayings. Between 1923 and 1941 he brought out sixteen numbered volumes for us.

Mody Boatright assisted Dobie in editing his last few volumes of our Publications. When Mody became editor-in-chief in 1943, he continued to take Dobie's view of the field of folklore as having no hard and fast boundaries. Mody wasn't a comparativist; his framework for folklore was American life and culture. He did not share Dobie's antipathy to the use of numbers for tale-types and motifs, but he did not introduce them into the volumes he edited. Emphasis still fell upon the collection of folklore rather than upon analysis or commentary.

When in the summer of 1951 Mody went to California to teach, he asked me to put together a volume out of the materials on hand. One of the large MSS consisted of a collection of Mexican folklore gathered in Austin by Soledad Pérez as a master's thesis under Mody's supervision. She worked with me in my office to add comparative notes and tale-type and motif numbers. The other large MS consisted of Ruth Dodson's tales about the marvelous cures of Don Pedrito Jaramillo, a famous curandero of the country around Falfurrias. When I asked Dobie for a contribution to the volume that was taking shape, he wrote an essay for it, "Charm in Mexican Folktales." I can't imagine that a folklorist of the Finnish school would have written on such a topic. I ventured to add two folktales which I had heard in Mexico and the volume was complete. When *The Healer of Los Olmos and Other Mexican Folklore* appeared in the fall, the comparative notes and the numbers were unobtrusive enough not to draw adverse comment from Dobie. In advance of publication Mody had approved of what I had done.

Before undertaking to do this editorial work at Mody's request, I had made a comparative study of a Mexican variant of the story of the bear's son which Dobie had incorporated in *Tongues of the Monte*. I told Dobie what I intended to do and gave him the MS to read before sending it off for publication—it did not even occur to me that it might find a place in a volume of the Society's. At the end of my paper I concluded that Dobie's Juan Oso story lacked certain elements which a comparison with other Spanish-American and European versions would lead one to expect. Two years later Dobie said suddenly to me at

Wilson M. Hudson

Barton Springs one hot afternoon that he remembered there was a part of the story which he didn't write down after hearing Ismael tell it. I am sure I didn't convert Dobie to the comparative method, nor was that my intention, but the fact that he didn't object to my article, which appeared in the *Southern Folklore Quarterly*, made me bold enough to publish several comparative essays of mine in later volumes of our Publications.

Mody insisted that *The Healer of Los Olmos* should show my name as sole editor, though I had no office in the Society. The next year he had Allen Maxwell and me elected associate editors—Allen was to be responsible for matters of typography and design. I regularly inserted numbers for tale-types and motifs wherever they were called for. And I also entered these numbers in the indexes of the Publications as they appeared volume by volume.

Why did I want to include tale-type numbers and motif numbers? Because it was evident that folklorists in general had been passing over our vast storehouse of materials for the reason that there was no ready way of locating variants in our Publications. Suppose a folklorist in England, Germany, or Italy was undertaking to study the myth of the birth of a people from a hole in the ground, chthonic birth, how would he know that an Alabama-Coushatta version of this ethnogenetic myth was recorded in *Mexican Border Ballads and Other Lore*? How would a Russian folklorist or a student of comparative literature discover that the story which Pushkin heard from his old nurse and which became the basis of the opera *Le Coq d'Or* has an analogue in the same un-likely place? I was proud of the Society's extensive and varied materi-als and chagrined at their neglect. It was too easily assumed that the Texas Folklore Society was concerned with strictly local manifesta-tions, that it was limited in its interests to Texas only. This was never true of us, from the time of our first volume down to the present day.

While Mody and I were editing the Publications together, there was an increase in the number of analytical and comparative articles; other-wise the content remained much the same. When I became editor in 1964 I made no noticeable changes. It seemed to me that none were called for. Our Publications were still enough in demand to be kept in print, all of them. What justification would there have been for me, acting on my own judgment, to alter the character of our Publications as determined by all of the preceding editors? I would not have "pro-fessionalized" our Publications even if that were possible. All I had wanted to do was to make room for the kind of article that would have been rejected in the earlier years, and this had been accomplished.

Mody and I now and then talked about the need for a general index that would make our materials easy to find and so would put research-ers all over the world in touch with the work and accomplishment of the Texas Folklore Society. Mody had had a student prepare an index, but it was sketchy and made no provision for the identification of tale-types or motifs. In time I persuaded Mr. James T. Bratcher, a graduate student at the University of Texas, to undertake a complete index that would be of the greatest use to a variety of scholars, folklorists first of all, but students of popular culture and historians as well. He would supply tale-type and motif numbers where none appeared in the text. After immense labor, Mr. Bratcher has completed the index and seen it through the press. At the present it is ready to be bound. Mr. Bratcher wished to have an advance copy to show us at our meeting this year, and he has succeeded in making the deadline. I now hold this copy in my hand—here it is. Southern Methodist University Press, whose imprint appears on many of our volumes, is publishing the in-dex for us.

We are very grateful to Mr. Leroy Brown, one of our members, who at our business meeting last year suggested that we approach the Moody Foundation for a grant to publish Mr. Bratcher's index. Since Mr. Brown was personally acquainted with the officer of the Founda-tion who receives applications for grants, he was able to give us as-sistance at all stages of our negotiations. To me it seems just short of miraculous that we should have applied for a grant, obtained it, and got the book into print within only one year.

The burden of filling out all the forms required by the Moody Foundation fell upon our present editor, Mr. Francis Edward Aber-nethy. At the close of the preface to the last book I edited for the Society, I expressed confidence that Mr. Abernethy would know how to make the best use of the productive energies of our Society, and now I want to reaffirm this confidence.

The professional folklorist sees folklore as something to be studied according to a systematic approach for the purpose of discovering some kind of knowledge relevant to it. The knowledge sought might concern its origin and dissemination, its structure, its bearing on ethnic history, or the light it sheds on the worldview or mental processes of the people to whom it belongs. The amateur sees folklore as a source of aesthetic pleasure, a means of transportation to a simpler and pleasanter state of being, a striking expression of folk wisdom, or a bizarre instance of folk imagination. It is hardly possible to be both a professional and an amateur folklorist at one and the same moment, but we can be professionals at one time and amateurs at another. We can enjoy the ballad of "Barbara Allen" and we can study it. It is very likely that those who choose to study do so because they first enjoyed. And retracing the historical course of a folktale does not spoil the pleasure we take in it. Knowledge may very well enhance enjoyment. It would be a pity if we were to become so professional that we should lose the amateur's attraction to folklore for its own sake. It would be a pity also if we were to suppose that folklore has no power to tell us anything about human beings and their group life.

One of the great strengths of the Texas Folklore Society at the present time is that we are a mixture of amateurs and professionals and no one feels that he has to be one or the other exclusively. There is no conflict. We have profited by the best aspects of both attitudes. May we continue to do so in the future.

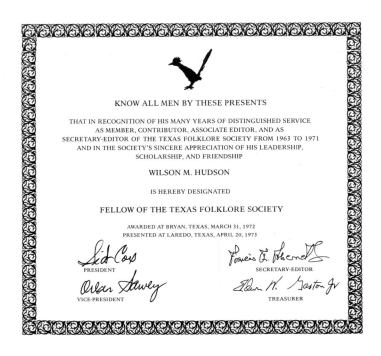

KNOW ALL MEN BY THESE PRESENTS

THAT IN RECOGNITION OF HIS MANY YEARS OF DISTINGUISHED SERVICE
AS MEMBER, CONTRIBUTOR, ASSOCIATE EDITOR, AND AS
SECRETARY-EDITOR OF THE TEXAS FOLKLORE SOCIETY FROM 1963 TO 1971
AND IN THE SOCIETY'S SINCERE APPRECIATION OF HIS LEADERSHIP,
SCHOLARSHIP, AND FRIENDSHIP

WILSON M. HUDSON

IS HEREBY DESIGNATED

FELLOW OF THE TEXAS FOLKLORE SOCIETY

AWARDED AT BRYAN, TEXAS, MARCH 31, 1972
PRESENTED AT LAREDO, TEXAS, APRIL 20, 1973

PRESIDENT   SECRETARY-EDITOR

VICE-PRESIDENT   TREASURER

SOME STILL DO
An Essay on Customs

CUSTOM involves the doing of things, doing them the same way at the same time in the same place. It can be as personal and as simple as the order of putting on one's shoes and socks, as practical as a spring roundup, or as social and complicated as Japanese rules of etiquette and conduct. But custom is always regular and it is always predictable because in the chancey ways of the world man has to have a solid base of things that he can depend upon, things tested and comfortable upon which he can settle his own shaky and luck-led life.

Before The Beginning all was without form. Then in the time of Creation the gods brought order out of chaos. They separated night from day and dry land from the ocean's water, and They established suns and seasons to live by and moons and months to plant and till and hunt by. And through it all They set a mighty heart beat that pulsed through the universe with a comforting regularity and made those suns and seasons and moons and months operate with a grand and beautiful—and dependable—rhythm.

On the other hand, the raw nature that emerged from this rhythmical whole seemed to be frighteningly whimsical and sanguine of claw. Although it operated from an ordered and dependable set of principles, its manifestations, as seen through the limited eye of man, were angry and incalculable, and his time was spent trying to establish an ordered life in the midst of the seeming disorder of floods and drouths, of fires and frosts. Since the beginning, every imaginable combination of catastrophe and calamity has hovered in the background of every culture and in the back of every mind, convincing man that even though he lived in God's ordered creation, Chance hovered in the background and could and would blow him away in the blink of an eye.

Custom, then, evolves from man's need for a stable, predictable, patterned way of life. He must be able to depend on the safeness of the paths he must daily walk, and he must be able to depend on tomorrow's being much like today. The chaos that man instinctively fears is closer to him than the storm overhead. It is in his wildly whirling, unpredictable and often uncontrollable mind and the thoughts that simmer there. It is in the very whirlwind of the explosive passions that he lives in the midst of, and he clutches frantically for something solid and dependable that he can hang on to. The more chaotic the mind and the times, the more necessarily solid must be the base. A neat and ordered mind can live in confusion. The normal, run-of-the-mill mind requires a place for everything and everything in its place. This "normal" mind expanded to include society itself—in times of disorder looks for something as totalitarianly solid as a Hitler in politics, as structurally solid as the caste system in society, and as fundamentally solid as medieval Catholicism in religion.

Custom, very loosely defined, consists of the habits men get into, the patterns by which they conduct their lives. A man's personal feeding, dressing, working, and playing habits become regularized parts of his life and he follows some of them with ritualistic regularity. A family gathers and worships and orders the structure of its membership and creates its own traditions and customs.

A man or a family might only frown when the customary order of things is violated; a society might possibly ostracize or execute the offending member.

Custom in the restricted definition of the term consists of the group's social conventions which have been established and sanctified by long tradition and which are enforced by social probation. Some are of such ancient vintage that time has erased their reasons for being. We veil our widows not remembering that this custom is the result of the belief that the spirits of the recently departed are envious of the living and would harm those nearest them if they are discovered. We rise, salute, genuflect, or prostrate ourselves in customary marks of obeisance to political and religious authority or to the symbols that stand for them. We close our businesses and quietly fast or noisily exhaust ourselves with sound and cymbal to celebrate the resurrection of a god and the springtime life and vegetation that accompanies this miraculous annual rebirth. And if we failed to do these things, to conduct ourselves according to the code and to celebrate the customary seasons and holidays, we would be uncomfortable in the patterns of our lives. We would have violated a part of our social conditioning.

Custom begins with two genetic drives or instincts that time and nature selected in man and other herd animals in order to promote their survival. These are the herding instinct and the instinct that causes us to fear the unfamiliar. The first, the sociality drive, or herding instinct, causes animals to cling together in groups for protection and propagation. For man, this herding instinct has multiplied his teeth and nails and has allowed a poorly armored and punily armed man to survive. Custom has as its purpose the solidifying of the group in singing and dancing together, in dressing and talking alike, in building and working together, and worshiping the same god in the same way. Custom is social cement, bonding a group into a social unit strong enough to survive.

The second instinct that gives rise to the practice of customs is man's negative reaction to the unfamiliar. Man the animal is either frightened by it and flees, or it activates his aggressive instincts. This is a survival quality. The animal that fails to react quickly and instinctively with fear or anger to the different and unfamiliar does not live to pass on his genes to another generation. Customs provide the familiar, and those who follow the customs and know the ways are insiders, are "The People." But those that don't are foreigners and strangers, and the group's ranks are tightly drawn up like a ring of musk oxen against the unfamiliarity of the outsider who might challenge or change the unity and sociality of the group.

These are the drives, constantly insisting that the herd band together, constantly fearful that something out of the ordinary will destroy the group's stability.

The urging of the instincts is strong and is undeniable and it is equally subtle, surfacing culturally in belief, in religions and tabus and superstitions that support what we only vaguely feel. Birth, death, and pain, strange comets and shooting stars, fearful storms, the unexplainable—therefore unnatural—occurrences that alter the normal order of things: these inspire our most conservative institutions, our religions which attempt to maintain the unchanging base from which our societies operate. And these inspire the rituals which go along with the religions, rituals with words and robes and altars and gestures that must be ever the same if they are to placate the evil that is forever among men—the evil, being that which violates the normal and understandable order of things.

Religion and the ritual that goes with it bonds man to his gods. Custom bonds man to man.

Some customs have changed little since man began because man has changed little. We still bow before dominance, celebrate the crossing of territorial bounds with ceremony, and cultivate elaborate rituals of courtship. Some customs have changed from literal to figurative actions. We no longer kill and eat the priests who are the hosts for the gods; we have wine and wafers instead. And we don't castrate the unworthy hunter; we cut off his shirt-tail.

Some customs change as society accumulates more knowledge. We have abandoned human sacrifice and we no longer have public hangings and no one goes to the king in search of a cure for the scrofula. In this same vein, the industrial revolution has also changed our ways of doing things, our customary methods of building and hunting and planting and living off the land. The old methods are abandoned in favor of more efficient ones. Old materials and tools give way to new. Horse-and-man power give way to the gasoline engine and electricity.

Some people, however, who know the old ways still practice them. They do so because the old ways are cheaper maybe, or simpler, or because they are just more comfortable with the old than with the new. The essays which follow deal mostly with this level of custom, with the doing of things in the old way.

Some people are still working stock, building chimneys, making syrup, curing warts, and witching water the same way their fathers and grandfathers did a hundred years ago. Some are still fiddling the same songs in the same way as did their ancestors, and they are still going to the same festivals and trade fairs that their people have been attending for generations. These things are the patterns of their culture's life, not to be ground under progress's wheel nor spun off by the whirling speed of life. These ways are the time honored customs of their lives, and though there might not be many who still know and follow some of these old ways, some still do.

FRANCIS EDWARD ABERNETHY
Nacogdoches, Texas
April 4, 1975

SOME STILL DO:
Essays on Texas Customs

WAGGONER'S COWBOYS

Photographs and text by
Francis Edward Abernethy

THE COWBOY is America's most representative and most market-able symbol. Stories about him and his songs and his styles are popu-lar from the Ginza to the Champs Elysees, and in the modern mind he has taken the place of the mounted knight on horseback. The cowboy image, even though it is frequently projected as a professional gun-fighter, has as sound a basis in history as his chivalric counterpart. He grew out of the working cowboy who came into being in Texas during the trail-driving days after the Civil War. He has come a long way since then and has made a greater impression on modern history and culture than has any other trade, craft, or profession.

The model for the modern cowboy symbol is not a complete figment of man's imagination. The best of his kind is alive with all the hoped-for virtues on the big ranches of West Texas. And some of the best of this geographically select group are on the six-county Waggoner ranch in north central Texas.

Dan Waggoner and his son Tom began building their herds in the 1850's, branding all the mavericks Dan and his men were tough enough to run down and throw. Dan and Tom and their cowboys fought Indians and drouths and competed with other stockmen for the accumulation of cattle and territory. In 1870 they trailed a herd to the Kansas railhead and made their first big financial profit, all of which they put back into a large spread and more cattle. They called this new ranch the Sachueista, after the Indian name for the tall grass that grew there. The Sachueista ranch is now over a hundred years old and getting stronger every year.

By the 1870's the boundary lines between cattle territories in West Texas had been pretty well agreed on, and it was up to the cowboys to see that the stock stayed on their own home range. After a long hard winter when the cattle had drifted uncontrolled in search of food and shelter, the cowboys from every spread in the area would gather for the spring round-up, where they would cut out their own stock and then drive them back to their home range. Dot Babb, an old-time Waggoner cowboy, said that during the 1880's it was not unusual to see twenty-five to thirty chuck wagons on the roundup grounds, each chuck wagon accommodating thirty to sixty men. That adds up to 1800 cowboys, if one works with maximums, and most of them stayed in West Texas and passed their genes and traditions on to their grandchildren and great-grandchildren, some of whom are today's cowboys. The world's present-day cowboy culture was shaped by the men who worked for the Waggoners, for Burk Burnett, Charles Goodnight, and Lum Slaughter, for the Four Sixes, the Matador, JA, and Pitchfork ranches, and this culture is as natural to West Texas as the cattle that still graze there.

There was a strong spirit among these men that formed a new kind of life on the cattle range. Even in the midst of their time and work they felt that they were different. They felt the heroic stance of their lives, and they played it up and made the most of it. Their pride in themselves and their unique and adventurous sorts of lives made up for the hardships they had to endure.

The mechanics of being a cowboy has changed some since those early days of D. Waggoner and Son, but the spirit is the same as it was. Waggoner's cowboys usually sleep in a bunkhouse that has a television set, but it is still in the cold of a dark morning that they are rousted out, loaded in the "dog wagon," and hauled to the chuck wagon fifteen or twenty miles away for breakfast. Another departure is that the chuck wagon isn't pulled by a team of mules anymore, and the hands don't have to depend on their hat brims for shade and protection from the weather when they eat and sleep at the wagon. The chuck wagon is now mounted on a big six-wheeled truck, and they cover it and the eating and sleeping area with a big tarpaulin. The food, however, is still cooked over mesquite coals in a pit or on an iron wood-stove, and the sounds that the cowboys hear at night when they sleep on the ground in bedrolls are the same sounds the old-timers heard—night hawks and coyotes, and the remuda as it grazes around them.

Getting ready to ride in the morning is the same as it always was. Two of the hands roll out before the rest, saddle up, and then drive up the hundred-horse remuda just as the day is lightening up. They push them into a holding pen that is made of one long rope braced waist high on stakes. These two hands then go to the wagon to eat, and two more cowboys rope out the horses to be used for the day.

These Three D horses are some of the best quarter horses in the world, all of them carrying the genes of carefully selected sires and dams. Each cowboy has a string of eight or ten horses which he is supposed to ride through fairly regularly and not wear out any one horse. They talk a lot about their horses and like them in direct proportion to how well they work. They aren't sentimental. They take care of their horses as a man takes care of his car, so they can get the most and best mileage out of them.

When Waggoner's cowboys are working a pasture many miles from the chuck wagon and a cattle truck is handy, they sometimes haul their horses to the work area in order to save time. Another thing that they have that their grandfathers didn't have is air support. When the pasture to be worked is extra large—and they sometimes call a two-thousand-plus-acre pasture a "trap"—the ranch foreman sends out a helicopter that herds the cattle from the back of the pasture up toward the pens where the cowboys are waiting. It would also surprise some of the old hands if they saw the cowboys roping from a jeep. But all that these modern methods do is to cut down on the number of cowboys needed to do the job. The work for each man is still the same. A cowboy on a horse ropes a calf and pulls him out of the bunch to be cut, notched, and branded in the same way as it has been since the beginning of cattle business.

No machine has been invented yet to gentle horses, either, and Wagonner's cowboys still break their own. Each January three or four hands are pulled off of cattle work to help the horse foreman break three-year-old broncs. These horses have spent their lives in the big pastures, and except for the times when they were branded and castrated they have never had a rope on them. Now they are roped, saddled, and ridden, and it speaks well for the bronc busters that a lot of horses go through with a minimum of acrobatics. Some do though and if skill can't keep the man on, then nerve has to get him up and make him get on again until he convinces the horse of the value of cooperation.

The Three D cowboys live a little better than the old hands did and they cover more territory, but essentially they are the same breed that worked with D. Waggoner and Son a hundred years ago. They have the skills, the nerve, the coordination, and endurance of professional athletes. Just about everything that a cowboy reaches for outweighs him and can run faster and hit harder than he can. It can hook him, tromp him, step on him, or kick a bone clean out of him, all of which it frequently does. The advantage the cowboy has is in direct proportion to the mastery of the skills of his profession.

This professional skill and their pride in it is one thing that separates Waggoner's cowboys from many other of the world's workers, most of whom do their jobs grudgingly or apologetically. The Sachueista men are cowboys because they want to be. Their pride and self-confidence is further bolstered by the knowledge that a large majority of the male population, young and old, USA-Europe-and-Asia, view them and their elite male-bond society with envy and admiration. Television, movies, literature, and advertising have pictured them as the national ego ideal, as symbols of the last line of battle against the depersonalization of the machine age and emasculation in an increasingly feminized society. An image which is that heroic can make up for long hours and low pay.

BUTTERMILK IS BEAUTIFUL

By Ernest B. Speck
Photographs by Tim Scheer

IN the years before REA and other invasions disrupted that simple pattern of life, the rural household in the Southwest had few pieces of equipment, and they were rudimentary in kind. Most of us are still familiar with some of the principal ones: the kerosene lamp; the wood-burning cookstove; the cabinet for storing dishes and left-over food (known as a "safe" because the doors on the upper part had screen wire to allow ventilation and to keep the contents safe from flies); the iron washpot in which were boiled the family wash, the lye soap with which to boil the clothes, water to scald the hogs before scraping them, and hog fat to produce lard and cracklings; the number three wash-tubs which served to cleanse both the family and its clothing; the solid iron smoothing irons which were heated on the cookstove or in the coals before the fireplace; and the heavy crockery, or stoneware, used for handling milk. It is this last item with which I wish to deal, more particularly one piece of this crockery, the churn, and the activities of which it was the center.

There was, of course, some variation from family to family in the handling of milk. What I shall describe is the way I knew on a sandy land farm in Llano County in west central Texas just before the demise of this part of folk life.

Before one can have milk and cream, one must have cows, or so we innocently thought forty years ago. The milk cow was as central to our way of life as rain. Not so romantic as her sisters of the range, the milk cow was equally as gaunt; we said she looked "drawed," for virtually all the nutriment she could get went into the production of calves and milk. In the winter in more prosperous times, she would be fed cotton seed and hay, but when the rains had failed us, she got corn shucks, top

15

fodder, nubbins, and mistletoe pulled from mesquite and hackberry trees. In the spring when the weeds began to grow, she ate so voraciously after her winter fast that the weeds caused her milk to have a bitter taste, especially if she had eaten much horehound. Although she usually calved in the spring, it was better that at least one or two cows be fresh in the fall to supply milk and butter through the winter. Our milk cows were not always of any particular breed, but if one showed signs of a Jersey strain, she was more elite and her milk was likely to be rich. Often she was brindled, her mammary endowment was rather small, but her milk was also rather rich. A cow which gave only "blue john," milk with little butterfat, was milked only if no other was available. Sometimes unruly, sometimes docile, a cow always submitted to milking more readily if she could chew on a stalk of top fodder at the same time. In fly time her tail was highly active; in late summer and fall her tail was a spiny club since the tassle was loaded with cockleburrs.

Perhaps the best place to start an account of the ritual of milk is at the birth of a calf. When a cow "found a calf," to use the euphemism we still employed, she would hide it in a clump of bee brush or chaparral and graze nearby. The trick was to get her to reveal the location of her calf by imitating a calf's bleat sufficiently well that she would rush to the calf to discover its difficulties. Since I was the best calf bleater available, this was one of the chores exclusively mine. Only once on our farm was there a case of difficult delivery. I found the cow, known to be due, in the throes of vain labor in a creek bottom. A neighbor, my father, and I played midwife, using as forceps a block and tackle designed for stretching fence wire.

The milk from a newly fresh cow was not used for several days. This is the period in which the milk is not good for human consumption because it contains, among other things, ingredients to stimulate the digestive tract of the calf. Most people waited for a week to ten days before using the milk. Usually after a week one could judge if the milk was good by observing the smell, color, texture, since it was darker and thicker and it smelled different from ordinary milk before it was good. Commercial dairies now wait at least three days to let the calf get the benefit of the antibodies, and then as soon as the calf is sold the milk is used. But it is then mixed with the milk of many cows in the cooling tanks. With only four or five other cows, and none of them record producers, we could not take that chance. Even though her milk was not used, the cow had to be milked twice daily, and the milk the calf could not drink was given directly to the pigs, whose digestion was sturdier than ours.

Once the milk was good, the milking pattern was fixed until the calf was weaned. Milk cows were not usually bred until the second time they came in heat after calving. This gave a longer milking period and produced bigger calves. Milking was rarely done by the major male members of the family. Younger boys were assigned the task, under pain of whipping if they did not do the job thoroughly. My father, meticulous in all things, would trust a good milk cow to no one else, for which I was grateful. It is essential that a cow be milked thoroughly, lest her production fall or she go dry. A good stripper was not one who divested herself of clothing in an enticing fashion, but one who could wring the last drops from a cow's udder, for the last drops were also the richest.

Before a cow was milked her calf was allowed to suck a little. The milker forced the calf to visit each of the teats. This process was necessary to "make the milk come down," as we said, to make it flow more readily. The calf would "hunch" the cow, that is push its nose rather violently into the udder, to encourage the flow of milk. When the calf seemed to be sucking contentedly no matter where its mouth was pushed, the calf was tied off while the cow was milked. Our cowlot was equipped with two mesquite trees, useful to tie calves to, but a fence post would serve as well. The loop on one end of the rope was passed around the calf's neck and then another loop was made by doubling the rope and passing it through the first loop and passing it around the calf's nose. This spread the pressure when the calf pulled on the rope so he would not choke himself and made release easy for one had only to slip the rope over his nose to set him free. If the calf were tied in front of the cow, she would lick it into some show of contentment while it waited to return to suck. Bull calves were generally more adamant, keeping the rope taut until they were released. We usually employed the three teat system, that is, we took three-fourths of the milk and left one-fourth for the calf to consume after we finished milking.

If one had two little pastures, as we did, the cows were turned into one and the calves into the other during the day. If there was but one pasture, the cows used it during the day, and the calves remained in the pen or lot (the terms were nearly interchangeable in our area), being given a chance to graze at night. The presence of the calves in so

Miss Ludell Ainsworth
Makes a Bait of Butter
Photographs by
Tim Scheer

handy a location during the day provided forbidden sport for farm boys. Calf-riding, with or without benefit of rope, presented a challenge few boys could resist, even though the unmistakable evidence of a fall in the cowlot often gave them away.

Milking was done into assorted kinds of containers, the principal one being the five-pound coffee bucket. (The word *pail* was never used in our area, although it was sufficiently well known that a German boy named Pehl was nicknamed "Bucket.") Whatever the type of bucket, galvanized, enameled, or coffee, it was used for milking and for nothing else. The milker squatted or kneeled, usually on one knee; if there was a milking stool in Llano County, I never heard of it. The milk was taken to the house where it was strained into gallon crockery bowls. The cloth through which the milk was strained to remove assorted barnyard impurities was of a coarse cotton variety, best provided by feed sacks which had contained "wheat shorts," ground wheat grain coverings rejected in the milling process, but a piece of ordinary flour sack that had been washed many times would serve.

The crocks were then placed in the "cooler," the nearest thing to refrigeration which we had. The cooler stood some four to five feet high and was made of galvanized sheet iron. Across the top was a pan about three inches deep, and around the upper edges of the pan were small nail-like spikes extending about a half-inch. Below the pan were usually three shelves, and at the bottom, a few inches above the floor, there was another pan. Four metal posts at the corners supported the pans and shelves. In operation the cooler was draped around with a large cloth which was attached to the spikes in the upper pan and extended to the lower pan. Water was placed in the upper pan and flowed down the cloth toward the lower pan. Evaporation of the moisture in the cloth provided the cooling for the milk. In our dry area the cloth would be moistened with a dipper several times a day, since evaporation was so rapid that the lower part of the cloth would otherwise never get damp. At night or in occasional damp spells, water actually flowed into the lower pan. But damp spells, except in the winter, brought thunder, and even though the temperature dropped, the milk soured, for everyone knows that thunder will sour milk.

Unless the weather was especially hot, the cooler would keep the milk from the night milking sweet until morning; the morning's milk usually stayed sweet until noon. For supper one had three choices of milk to drink: blinky or, more usually, clabbered milk from the morning milking, warm milk recently brought in from the cowlot, or butter-milk from that day's churning. Clabber was most often the choice. After the cream had risen and been "skum" off into another crock, there remained the curdled milk, rich in solids, sour in taste, lumpy in consistency, but refreshing to the palate of a work-weary man. Miss Muffet called it her curds and whey. Although there were those who sugared their clabber, we hardy souls welcomed its bite.

We come now to the feature of the milk complex which to us was pre-eminent. There were those more knowledgeable than my fore-bears who made clabber into smear-case or cottage cheese, or those who dolloped sour cream into assorted preparations. In our Anglo-Saxon innocence (my German heritage had been lost several genera-tions back) we made butter. And for the making of butter the tool was, of course, the churn. It was another piece of heavy crockery, varying in size from two to five gallons in capacity. Wooden churns were common somewhat earlier. Its sides bulged in barrel-like fashion, and at the top there was another more abrupt bulge to form a cup-like lip into which the lid fit. The lid had in its center a hole through which the dasher passed. The churn dasher was made of three pieces of wood: a long handle, somewhat like a broom handle, at the lower end of which two short rectangular pieces were attached in the form of cross which agitated the liquid in the churn as the dasher was moved up and down. We knew of more sophisticated churns that operated with a crank which turned paddles, but we eschewed many such contraptions. I suspect we felt they were somewhat effete chiefly because we could not afford them. And mechanical separators to separate the cream be-fore it had time to rise were not common in our area at the time.

The liquid in the churn consisted of cream and some clabber, the latter added to increase the bulk. Ideally it should be slightly cool, so churning was usually done in the morning. Churning took various lengths of time. One of my uncles who as a boy often churned said one thousand strokes of the dasher were needed. I have not been able to determine if the expression, "change hands and never miss a stroke" had its origin beside a churn, but that seems a likely place. If the butter was slow in congealing, a little cool water was added to encourage the process. The practiced churner was one who could move the dasher up and down in methodical rhythm, never lifting it high enough that the cross pieces came out of the liquid, for re-entry caused a messy splash despite the lid.

Churning was another job given to lesser members of the household, since it was a monotonous task. My grandmother did our churning for years. My mother, ever alert to the exigencies of life, timed the readying of the churn with care. She never found time to get the churn ready until she was sure my grandmother had finished her after-breakfast dip of snuff. Grandma dipped tooth-brush fashion, that is she used a piece of mesquite root sufficiently chewed on one end to form a brush-like collection of fibers. The moistened fibers were then dipped into Levi Garrett's, and the snuff was thus conveyed to the mouth. Obviously it was better that she not be dipping as she sat over the churn. Let it be said that Grandma decried her snuff-dipping. She felt it beneath her Carolina heritage and a vulgar practice to be blamed on her father's foolish move to Texas before the Civil War.

Before I take butter to its next stage, I should like to digress for just a moment. My grandmother, in her attempts to preserve what she believed to be Carolina niceties, was circumspect in her use of language about the cattle. If she ever referred to the appendages on a cow's udder, I don't recall ever hearing it. If our bull, when we had one, disturbed her by bellowing and kicking up dust as she worked with her beloved roses in the front yard, she would call me to "run that old male away." A bull was also euphemistically called "Old Surly." When the male calves or shoats were being castrated, she kept strictly to her room, and if forced to speak of the operation, she would say that the men were, not "altering," but "arranging" the stock.

Although anyone could hear the change in sound of the liquid in a churn when the butter came, it took a practiced eye to determine that a proper amount in terms of the contents of the churn had been produced. When it appeared that all of the fat in a churning had congealed, the butter was gathered by rotating and raising and lowering the dasher slowly. Then it was spooned out into a crock. It was worked with a spoon to force out all the whey which still remained. Salting the butter came next, and again it was a matter of practice which guided the butter-maker. My mother's system was to look at the mound of butter, shake from the box what she considered to be an appropriate amount of salt into one palm and as she worked the butter with the other hand, slowly sift in the salt. Once the butter had been worked and salted, and tasted, it could be treated in either of two ways. The less fancy way was to heap it in mounds in bowls. We had a butter mold, a wooden device of two parts. One part consisted of a rectangular box minus a lid, the bottom of which had a round hole a half-inch or more in diameter. The other part was a flat piece of wood which fit into the box and to which was attached a short round handle that extended through the hole in the box. The two parts were assembled, and the butter was packed into the box. The butter press was then inverted over a shallow bowl or plate, or a piece of grease-proof paper, the handle was pushed, and a more or less rectangular glob of butter, weighing around a pound, fell onto the plate or paper. Butter placed on paper was wrapped and sold in town. Butter sales were often the source of my money for nickel sacks of tobacco. The butter on plates was put in the cooler for our consumption.

Perhaps there is no need to mention the uses of butter, they are so numerous, but there are a few I should like to dwell on. Since we cooked our own bread, or rather Mother did, hot bread necessitated butter, whether the bread was the biscuits we had for breakfast or the cornbread we had for dinner, at noon. At night, cold biscuits and cornbread likewise tasted better with butter. If the bread was not hot, sorghum molasses could be mixed with butter and lifted to the bread with the knife that mixed them to create a different taste and textural sensation. Needless to say layer cakes and the large soft cookies we called tea-cakes baked with butter were rich in flavor and cholesterol.

Since butter was a salable product, some people skimped on their use of it to earn a few extra pennies. But this was not a condoned practice. A most condemnatory bit of gossip concerned the man two farms up the creek who fed his children salted lard so that he might sell his butter.

The by-product, so to speak, of butter-making was, of course, butter-milk. A day or two older than clabbered milk, it had more bite to it. But its texture was smoother and the tiny globules of butter that one found made it seem even smoother. It has long been my contention that the step from buttermilk, with its combined bite and smoothness, to bourbon and branch water is a short one, decreed of the gods.

But there are other virtues to be attributed to buttermilk. It was, and in its machine-made form still is, a basic ingredient in cooking. Buttermilk pies, with one crust and no meringue, were a favorite. Proper biscuits and cornbread could not be made with anything but buttermilk. Cornbread made with buttermilk, home-boiled lard, and meal fresh from the local grist mill never had the consistency of library paste and sand that the modern product has. Buttermilk also served as the principal ingredient in salad dressing, along with salt and pepper. (The proper makings for such a salad were leaf lettuce, mustard leaves, green onions, and radishes.) The infant who could handle neither its own mother's milk nor fresh sweet milk from a cow would often thrive on buttermilk. The natural partner for certain foods, such as cornbread and turnip greens, was buttermilk. Although folk belief prohibited the drinking of milk with fish, this prohibition often did not apply to buttermilk.

It was reputed to have cosmetic properties. In a day when white skin rather than a suntan was a mark of sophistication, buttermilk was used to protect the skin when exposure to the sun was unavoidable. And it was believed useful in removing skin blemishes of any sort. A facial pack of buttermilk and oatmeal or cornmeal was used to cleanse, bleach, and soften the skin. There was even a soap made of buttermilk. And buttermilk could bring relief in cases of sunburn.

No less an authority than Mody Boatright once recommended buttermilk to me for diarrhea for it could calm the agitation in a rumbling gut. Whether one suffered from hangover, grief, or insomnia, buttermilk, sometimes accompanied by a piece of cornbread, could relax one's innards and soothe his soul far beyond the reaches of any pharmaceutical concoction of our day. Indeed, buttermilk is beautiful.

MAKING SYRUP

As told by Eugene Martin

Photographs by F. E. Abernethy

1. A lot of people are going back to making syrup because of the high price of sweetening. This here's some we made in October in 1973, here in Nacogdoches. I built that old furnace—or helped build it—and put the mill up. I got that mill and the copper pan from Mr. Henry Hoya when I bought this place back in '36. For a while these last years we didn't make much syrup; it wasn't worth planting the cane for. But we're really going to make some syrup this fall.

25

2. That tractor's doing what it used to take two good mules to do. I'm turning the mill there. That's a big mill, called a Big Fourteen, and it can squeeze out a lot of juice if you feed it right. That's Mr. John Jenkins feeding the mill and Mr. Josh is on the other side pulling the baggings so they won't get all piled up.

3. Mr. Jenkins is feeding the mill. It was his cane that we were using that day. He was getting behind poking the cane. You can get eight or ten pieces of ribbon cane in the Big Fourteen if you know how. A little mill will only take three or four. It takes about eighty stalks of ribbon cane—takes more of sorghum—to make a gallon of juice, and it takes about eight gallons of juice to make a gallon of syrup. So you see you've got to raise a lot of cane if you're planning to go in the syrup business.

4. The juice comes out of the mill and holds in the juice box. The juice box is made out of cypress; there's an old hen setting in it right now. You hold the juice in the box until they're ready for it at the pan. Then you open the faucet at the pan and let the juice flow in. You can see the pipe there that carries the juice down to the starting end of the pan.

5. That's Mitch Curl feeding the fire. He's feeding fat pine. That's the best wood 'cause it gets a good blaze going that's big enough to draw up over the duck's nest in the middle of the furnace and then shoot on down in the hole at the far end and on out the smoke stack. The heat from a good fat pine fire that's really drawing well is hot and steady from one end of the pan to the other.

6. That's the pan. Really that's an evaporator. The old folks used a pan, and they had to dip the juice from one part of the pan to the next. Now the juice pours into one end of the evaporator and the heat causes it to circulate and move from one end to the other. By the time it gets to the other end it's made syrup. It takes about an hour of cooking to do that.

7. They're skimming the juice. That's Mr. Buck Sanders and Mitch throwing off the skimmings. And you can see where the syrup drains off at the smoke stack end of the pan and pours into that tub there. When they get enough syrup in the tub, they start filling up those half-gallon cans. They're getting a pretty good price for syrup nowadays. Sure makes it worth doing.

ARDEN HOOKS, BIG THICKET BEE COURSER

Photographs and Text by Ralph Ramos

BEES live in successful communism, making it work because each bee puts out his best effort. Humans can't make a success of communism because not everyone would make such an effort. How's that for a bit of piney woods observation and philosophy? It came from Arden Hooks who ought to know about bees and men. He's been around both for a whole lot of years.

Arden Hooks is of a fading breed of men known as "bee coursers." There never were many of them and there are just about none at all nowadays. A "bee courser" is a fellow endowed with keen eyesight, a built-in range-finding sense, and enduring patience. He observes honey bees at their work, watches them fly off, plots their course and then painstakingly trails them to some bee tree hidden in the most secluded and thickety portions of the forest. Success is measured in buckets of fresh, wild honey robbed from the trees the courser finds. Hooks' best year came eight years ago when he trailed bees to thirty trees.

Alex Work, another bee man and expert in an even more difficult tracking endeavor, that of coursing hornets, is going to put out a couple of bee hives at Hooks' camp on Cypress Creek. Of which Hooks explains, "I'm hoping the bees will separate and swarm, buzz off and build new hives in hollow trees here on my place. Then I can course them until I'm tired."

He has already determined where the bees are going that have started working in his clearing. The courses of three or four different sets of bees go off to domestic bee hives. But there are two sets of wild bees. The flight line of one set moves about fifteen degrees east of north and Hooks figures there's a bee tree somewhere out there, "Somewhere in Tom Coe's bottom." The other flight line is southeasterly. Hooks has coursed that flight a long time and says, "It goes into an isolated section down toward the T. and N.O. trestle. There'll be a bee tree there." Here's the way Hooks goes about it, making it sound a whole lot easier than it is: First he'll put out a bait of honey in a half-pound coffee can. Inside the can he'll float sticks on the honey so bees dipping in for sweets won't drown. The can he'll put up in a clearing. To get a bee's attention Hooks will then sprinkle a mix of honey and water on nearby foliage, preferably on sweet gum leaves.

Once a bee locates the bait of honey he'll go to it to load up for delivery to his hive. Hooks observes as the bee buzzes heavily laden out of the can. It'll circle two or three times for orientation purposes then take off toward the hive or bee tree.

Usually, he'll tell you, the bee will take the shortest distance to his lair and that's where we got the expression "bee line." Sometimes, though, the bee will put a courser off the track with a well designed detour. Hooks explains, "If there happens to be a right-of-way nearby and in the general direction of the bee's destination, he'll take it. Flying is easier. It don't take much of a right-of-way either. I've seen them follow old hacked out land lines. When the bee gets near his hive he'll make a ninety degree turn and fly right straight to it."

As he talks on, Hooks chuckles to himself and occasionally comes out with wisdom like, "Bee coursing is sort of like an adult Easter egg hunt."

Easiest way to course a bee, he'll tell you, is to find him watering. He'll make a bee line to his tree from there. What Hooks does is to figure that flight course as the bee leaves bait or watering hole. He doesn't use a compass, depending instead on the sun. He'll walk about a quarter mile, what he calls "a reasonable distance." If the bee doesn't zoom on past, Hooks will start back, looking for an opening into which the honey-maker may have flown. If he loses the bee completely he'll move the bait into another small clearing and watch.

"That way," Hooks reveals, "I can get a new bearing on the bee's course and by triangulation know just about where he's going."

He has a trick to try on difficult coursing. He'll trap a bee inside the bait can by flipping a handkerchief over the top. He then picks up the can and its trapped bee and walks off in the direction he has plotted. When he figures he has walked far enough he uncovers the can and the bee will head right straight to his tree.

At the tree the bee will go into his dance where he communicates with the other workers. It doesn't take long for him to get out the word

and before long there's a steady stream of bees going and coming.

He can figure, too, just about how far away a bee tree is. Says Hooks, "Watch that first bee; he's the important one. If it takes him six minutes to leave the can and return, the tree will be close to a quarter of a mile away. If it takes twelve minutes figure between a quarter and three quarters. That'll help give you your guide."

The reason that first bee is so important, Hooks says, is because he'll make two or three trips solo before the other bees start flying in and out.

He sort of gauges the distance by noting how fast the bee flights build up. "If the tree is close the number of bees traveling will build up rapidly." He'll tell you, too, that if the bee tree is a long way off it may take two or three days before that first bee comes buzzing in to the bait can. He figures it takes bees about thirty minutes to get their course straightened out and after that the flight path is definite.

Even knowing just about where the bees are making and storing their honey it's sometimes difficult to pinpoint the exact tree. "They're pretty elusive. You can look your eyes out, pass right under the tree and go past it. Then if you're observant enough you will note that the course of bees passing you is the reverse from the course you're on. So you turn around and start back. You've sure enough missed the tree.

"The best way to spot a tree is to face the sun when you look over a suspicious tree. That way you can spot the bees if they're there. Or get up close to the suspicious tree and look straight up the trunk. Foliage won't get in your way. If they're there you can see where they go into the main trunk."

If it's hot summertime July, Hooks often spots them by sound. "They get noisy then. Maybe it's because there's a July crop of young bees and they're busy carrying water to them. They need a lot of water.

"And if it's good and hot you'll find a lot of bees at the bee tree opening, fanning it with their wings to provide cooling ventilation for the workers and young and the queen inside."

Hooks won't help rob the tree. "I leave that up to Alec, L. G. Roberts, and Jerry Anderson. I take them to the tree, but I make sure I'm standing off a safe distance. I don't like being stung."

When they rob a tree the men will throw it so the tree won't be broken too much. They'll then try to stop up the entry hole to seal the bees in while they work. Cuts are then sawed half way through the tree above and below the entry hole. Using an axe or a wedge the plug is then split out to uncover the cache of honey inside.

"They get anywhere from two or three cups full of honey to a tubful."

Hooks gets the pleasure of finding the tree and, for pay, enough old honey for bait another time.

Over his years of bee coursing and listening to the tales told by his father, Henry Allen Hooks, and his uncle, Ben Hooks, Arden Hooks is a walking encyclopedia of such bee lore as the following.

If it's a rainy spring and early summer bees don't work and don't make much honey. If it's a dry spring it'll be a good honey-making year. If winters are too cold bees will die. If their entry holes are too big, they're not protected and will freeze.

Most bee men will try to tell you that bees use holes only on the south side of the tree. Hooks' observation is that there seems to be no rule. They'll use holes anywhere if they lead to a hollow. Usually bees will use natural holes, but Hooks has found that where a tree cutter has sawed into a cavity and quit, the bees will use the saw cut for an entry.

Sometimes bees will swarm several times in a summer. Normally they'll do it only once and usually in April. Give them a month to work, then rob the bee tree in May.

If a swarm of bees is prosperous, that is making plenty of honey, it will break up and swarm to find a new tree. Where their queen goes they'll settle. On the other hand, if it's not a prosperous year they won't swarm. Maybe in bad times they kill off any new queens which come along.

Hooks is curious about one thing which years of observation haven't told him. Do the bees scout out a new location before or after they swarm?

Hooks has been stung a time or two, usually while putting out bait or moving it. "They won't sting you while they're feeding. And as mean a reputation as the hornet has he won't sting while eating either. But let a bee get tangled in the hair on your arm and he'll get irritated right now and sting you."

He's positive about one thing, saying, "Bees won't work when the temperature is below sixty degrees. They're as good as a thermometer about that." Bees know, too, when it's going to rain. "I've observed bees coming into a hive or tree and not leaving as they normally would. When that occurs it won't be long before a sudden thunderstorm will come up. They won't go back to work until the threat of more rain is gone. You can depend on it."

There are fewer hives and trees are dying out. Hooks notes, "There's not as many bees as there used to be." He doesn't blame insecticides believing the bee trees are too deep in the woods to be affected. There are diseases spreading, the web worm gets a lot of bees, and if it is too wet bees starve to death.

Even so there are plenty of wild bees left for the coursers to follow. Hooks figures the Railroad Commission might be governing them because he has found them spaced just like oil wells, one every forty acres. At least that's the way it is on the section of land he stomps regularly.

Strange pastime? Maybe so but to Arden Hooks and the few others who course bees "It beats the devil out of playing golf."

Reprinted by permission, *Beaumont Enterprise*, March 9, 1975.

TRADITION AND THE CANDELILLA WAX INDUSTRY

Photographs and Text by Joe S. Graham

THE candelilla wax industry, like the guayule rubber industry, is almost unknown in the United States, outside of the trans-Pecos region of West Texas. Few visitors to the area are exposed to what has been an industry of considerable consequence in the past, and is certainly one of the most fascinating in the area. Most of the residents of the Big Bend region know something about the candelilla wax industry because of the many articles about it which appeared in local newspapers during the period from 1930 to 1950. Since that time, however, one does not read or hear much about it because it has declined greatly in importance, another casualty to modern technology.

The first wax production in West Texas began sometime during the second decade of this century and blossomed into a multi-million dollar industry during the 1920's, 1930's and 1940's. With the drop in price in the early fifties the industry fell on hard times and has never recovered, though production still goes in the area—mostly in Mexico at present. Another factor in the decline of the industry is that technology has produced a synthetic substitute for about one-fourth the cost of candelilla wax. So where once there were hundreds of wax camps scattered up and down the Rio Grande in the 1930's and 1940's, now there are no more than a few dozen, and at times there are none producing wax on the Texas side. As a result of the activity in the past, however, one frequently encounters those who have worked in wax camps—both Anglo and Mexican American.

For the uninitiated, candelilla wax is a natural wax taken from the plants of the Euphorbicaeae family, principally *Euphorbia Antisphilitica* (so named because of the folk belief that the acidic, milky juice of the plant was a cure for syphilis), *Euphorbia Ceriform*, and

39

Pedilanthus Pavonis. Candelilla means "little candle," and the name indicates one of its uses—making candles. Centuries ago this wax was used to waterproof leather; during World War II it was used extensively to waterproof army tents. The natives of Mexico have used it for hundreds of years in making amulets and figurines. It now has well over a hundred uses, among them waxes and polishes for shoes, cars, and floors, and even as a base for chewing gum. It is used in tanning leather, in cosmetics, and in phonograph records. Two of the largest consumers of candelilla wax in the United States reportedly are the Johnson Wax Company and Wrigley's (gum) Inc.

In 1954, 95% of the world's supply of this wax was produced in five of Mexico's hottest, driest states: Coahuila, Nuevo León, Chihuahua, Durango, and Zacatecas. Most of the rest was produced in West Texas, in four of the state's hottest and driest counties: Presidio, Brewster, Terrell, and Val Verde. It is ironic that this harsh region, which ranges in altitude from 3,000 to 6,000 feet above sea level, whose temperature varies from more than 110° F on summer afternoons down to nearly 0° F on early winter mornings, and whose annual rainfall is less than two inches in places, produces plants which give the highest wax yield. In areas with more favorable climate the plant may grow to gigantic proportions—as high as nine feet in the Dallas area—but it produces almost no wax and consequently is commercially unexploited. In order to produce wax, the plant must grow in the hot, dry climate found in north-central Mexico and in West Texas because the plant, in order to survive in this environment, forms a heavy wax coating along its stems to prevent moisture loss and to protect it from the cold. The hottest, driest summers and coldest winters produce plants with the most abundant wax.

At present, almost all of the wax shipped from West Texas is brought over from Mexico because it is easier to import than to produce on this side. "Import" is the proper word because it is not illegal to bring the wax into this country (indeed, there is not even an import duty). It is, however, illegal to export the wax from Mexico without channeling it through the *Banco de Mexico* so that the export tax can be collected. Thus, for the American it is importing; for the Mexican wax maker it is smuggling.

There are two ways that the wax gets to the border. Smugglers bring burro pack trains loaded with raw wax from the interior of Mexico, sometimes as far as 150 miles. Most of this wax finds its way into Lajitas, Texas, a few miles up river from the Big Bend National Park. Here the smugglers sell their wax, buy badly needed supplies, and disappear back into Mexico. These men are full-time smugglers, clandestinely buying the wax in Mexico and selling it in Texas at a good profit. As long as the *mordida* (or bribe, part of the Mexican way of life, particularly along the border) is paid, these men go unmolested.

The other source of wax is the small producer who lives in camps along the Rio Grande. These wax camps usually are made up of from two to six men who produce the wax and bring it across the river on burros or in small boats. Each man, either by himself or with a partner, is an entrepreneur who works for himself and receives no wages. It is this group that is of interest in this paper.

Perhaps I should explain briefly how I came to know about candelilla wax making. My father was a River Rider from 1947 to 1954. A River Rider was one who patrolled the Rio Grande on horseback for the Federal Government to keep animals from crossing into the United States during the hoof-and-mouth epidemic in Mexico. During this period of time our family lived in camp with my father (I say camp because few River Riders had houses to live in, and army tents were more common) during the summer months after school had ended. For three of these summers our camp was located a stone's throw from a large wax camp on the Texas side, and my younger brother and I spent most of every day with the Mexican wax makers. Eighteen years later, after I joined the faculty at Sul Ross, I had the opportunity to renew my acquaintance with the wax camps while making a documentary film (funded by a Sul Ross research grant) of the industry. This time I was able to observe through the eyes of a folklorist.

By any standard or definition these candelilla wax makers comprise a distinct folk group, in this case an occupational group. Much of the folklore of this group is unique only in that it deals with the occupation and its hazards (primarily getting arrested by the *federales* when the *mordida* (bribe) is not paid. Anyone who has read Oscar Lewis' *Tepoztlán* knows the cultural background of these men. They are neither ambitious nor inventive, as we normally think of the terms; they are neither lazy nor stupid. They possess an esoteric knowledge pertaining to their occupation, which helps to form them into a fluid though cohesive group, isolated from other members of society for long periods of time.

They learn to make wax through apprenticeship, often beginning as early as twelve years old on one of the ranches in the interior of Mexico. By the time they come to the border they usually have all of the knowledge required to gather and process the plant. They do not work for wages here as they did in the interior; they are business-men—they gather, process and sell the wax, and their wages are their profits. The harder they work, the more they make. Most of these men earn almost twice the average wage for a laborer in this area, aver-aging about $4.00 per day. To see how this business is operated, we shall observe one man, Antonio Avila, as he produces candelilla wax.

Like many of his compadres, Antonio is functionally illiterate; hav-ing no formal education, he writes his name with effort. And like the rest of the local population, Antonio relies on the same folk cures and remedies that his ancestors relied upon. He uses a tea made of the *cenizo* plant for a chronic stomach ailment; he is not sure what the problem is, for it has been years since he has seen a *médico*. At forty-two Antonio is married and has three children, but they live over a hundred miles away in Durango. This summer he has a four-teen-year-old nephew, Juan Valencia, helping him. Juan thinks that making wax may be fine as a summer job, but he is convinced that an education offers him a better future. Antonio and Juan share the camp with Gregorio Martínez, a taciturn man who works by himself. Gregorio's right leg was severed in an auto accident ten or eleven years ago and he has a peg leg from the knee down. He would like a job on one of the large ranches in Texas because, as he explains, *"es más fácil,"* it is easier. Making candelilla wax helps provide for *both* of his wives, one in Boquillas and one in Juárez.

The other resident in the camp is Phillippe Madrid, whose wife died three years ago and left him with seven boys. The three young-est, ages six, eight and eleven, live in camp with him. The eleven-year-old helps with the wax processing, but the two younger boys spend their time hunting lizards, June bugs, and an occasional bird with their sling shots.

Antonio lives a life of such simplicity that Thoreau's Walden is a Statler-Hilton by comparison; one significant difference, however, is that Thoreau could leave anytime he wanted to—Antonio cannot. He cooks over a campfire with the barest of utensils: one tin skillet and the top cut from a fifty-five-gallon steel drum placed over hot coals to cook his flour tortillas on. He hauls his drinking water from the river in a five-gallon bucket with a Fina oil products label on it. If the river is muddy, he lets the water settle for a few minutes before drinking it. His diet consists of flour tortillas, beans, coffee, sugar, onions, chiles, and vermicelli. He could have fish, but he usually doesn't take the time to catch them. He has little or no shelter from the elements because he really doesn't need it. All of his belongings fit easily into one cardboard box.

Antonio rises from his bed (usually located in one of the stacks of unprocessed candelilla plant, or *yerba*) shortly after sunrise and gets about the day's affairs. He makes strong coffee on the open fire and sips this from a tin cup as he prepares breakfast, usually beans in some form with hot chile and flour tortillas. He mixes enough dough to make enough tortillas for the whole day, then patiently rolls them out on a piece of board and cooks them on his make-shift grill. When breakfast is over, he wipes his utensils clean and begins his day's work—we could say a week's work, or a month's work, or even a year's work, because there is little variation. He must take his burro out into the rugged mountains along the river in search of the candelilla plant. When he finds enough of the *yerba*, he must pull it by hand, tie it into bundles, bring it into camp on burros, stack it, and then process it. Once the wax is processed, he must then smuggle it across into Texas and sell it to the local refiner. After selling his wax, he buys the necessary staples from the small store near the refinery and goes back to camp to repeat the cycle.

Antonio's life is not run by the clock, and he seems the happier for it. The whole time I have been among these men I don't recall having seen a watch or clock. Only if he works for an Anglo must Antonio concern himself with the time of day. Looking through his ethnocentric bias, the Anglo sees Antonio as lazy and indolent. Antonio simply marches to another drum. His concept of time differs from that of the Anglo, upon whom he looks with disdain through his own ethnocentric bias. For him, time, like any good Mexican clock, walks; it doesn't run. When he feels that it is time to arise, he does so, without relying on a clock to tell him when; when it is time to work, he works; and when it is time to rest, he rests.

Antonio's first task after eating is to locate his four burros, which is no great problem even though they are not in a corral, because he has hobbled them the night before. He removes the hobbles and drives the animals into camp and saddles them. He uses no bridles and the blankets he uses to protect the burros' backs from the pack saddles are nothing but worn-out gunny sacks. His saddles may either be handmade or bought from one of the small stores along the river.

After saddling his burro, Antonio places one of the modern technological miracles onto one of his saddles—a half-gallon plastic Clorox bottle filled with river water. He then jumps astride one of the burros, behind the saddle of course, since the human posterior is not designed to be draped over a pack saddle. He leaves camp in search of candelilla. He may have to travel as far as five miles, depending on how long the camp has been operating. The older the camp, the farther he has to go to get to the weed.

When he locates sufficient candelilla, Antonio stops his burros and hobbles them, leaving them free to search for what food is available in the area nearby. He learned many years ago how to turn a two-foot piece of grass rope into an effective hobble. The center of the rope is placed above the hoof of the foot opposite where Antonio is squatting. He pulls the rope around the leg and twists it eight or nine times. The two short ends then are placed around the burro's other leg, just above the hoof, and the large knot on one end is pushed through the braid of the other end.

Once the burros are hobbled, Antonio takes the ropes used to tie the *yerba* into bundles and gives half of them to his fourteen-year-old nephew. These ropes are about twelve feet long, with a loop at one end which is either lined with leather or made of wood. The wooden loop consists of a short U-shaped piece of wood fastened to the rope. It is simple, effective, and durable. There are four ropes for each burro.

Then the real work begins. Antonio stretches the rope out along the ground near several large clumps of the candelilla plant. He then proceeds to pull the weed, which grows to a height of about eighteen inches. The only technique thus far developed for pulling the weed is the grunt and heave method. Antonio learned long ago that he could not cut the weed, because the roots would bleed to death. If pulled up by the roots, however, the plant will grow back in even greater abundance in five or six years, ready for another harvest. He has also learned that the plants, after pulling, must be stacked properly or the bundles will not last until he gets to camp. When he has gathered enough *yerba* for one bundle—about forty to fifty pounds—he then ties it. There must be a hundred different ways to tie a bundle of candelilla, but of the many men I have observed working with candelilla, all have used the exact same steps and have tied the exact same knot.

My experience teaching college freshmen to write process papers convinces me to avoid attempting to describe in detail the mechanics of tying this particular knot. Suffice it to say that the process of tying the bundle and the knot used are masterpieces of efficiency. Certainly it is as complex as throwing a diamond hitch, which is almost a lost art. The rope passes twice around the bundle to hold it secure. The knot is so tied that it can be suspended on the pack saddle and not slip, yet when the bundle is placed into the stack at camp, a single pull unties the knot and removes the rope from the bundle. None of the men could tell me who invented the knot; they could tell me only where they learned to use it. Though some among us, through trial and error, might develop an equally successful way to tie the candelilla into bundles, we doubtfully could invent one more effective or efficient. For Antonio, who is not particularly inventive by our standards, it is a simple process—use the technique tried and tested by generations of wax makers.

Once the bundles are tied, four for each burro, they are loaded and hauled into camp and stacked. Once Antonio has one hundred *cargas* (bundles) of the candelilla plant, he may take his turn at the vat. Since the vat does not belong to these men (it belongs to the purchaser and refiner of the wax), they have worked out this system for sharing it.

The equipment used in boiling the plant is minimal—enough but just barely. The one piece of equipment especially made for wax producers is the *paila*, a steel vat which is about eight feet long, four feet wide, and four feet deep (the size of the vat differs from one camp to another). The *paila* is covered with a heavy removable grate. It is set into the river bank with a space for the fire beneath it. Besides the vat, Antonio's equipment consists of two pitchforks, two fifty-five-gallon barrels, two or three five-gallon buckets, an *espumador* (a shallow, sieve-like scoop), an urn or glass jar containing sulfuric acid, and a *bote para el ácido* (a can or jar attached to a stick used to pour the acid into the vat with). Sometimes there is a *chivo* (literally goat, but in this case a stick about four feet long with a small fork on the end which resembles a billy goat's horns) which is used to push protruding ends of the candelilla below the surface of the water after the grate has been fastened into place. The *espumador, bote para el ácido*, and *chivo* are handmade. *Espumadores* differ only in size: they are made of a round or oval, dish-shaped piece of sheet metal with many fairly large nail holes punched through it making it resemble a sieve. A round wooden handle, usually a piece of tree limb, is attached to the metal. Making *espumadores* is like tying bundles of candelilla—it is simple if someone has shown you how. The *espumador* is used to skim the molten wax which rises to the surface of the water during the boiling process, and the holes allow most of the water to escape back into the vat. It would be hard to conceive of a simpler but more effective tool. Again, Antonio does not have to invent this or to depend upon a store to furnish this piece of equipment. Somewhere he has learned to make *espumadores* and is the more self-sufficient for it.

Anyone who has had even elementary chemistry knows that when one pours concentrated sulfuric acid into water there is a violent, boiling reaction. Antonio uses the hand-made *bote para el ácido* to pour the acid into the vat of water without being splattered by the acid. Like the *espumador*, this implement resembles almost every other one. It consists of a small "tin" can or glass jar fastened to a stick with a piece of bailing wire; this is done in one of two ways: Either the container is placed in the fork of a stick or it is simply wired onto the side of a straight stick.

Cooking the wax is the most tedious and difficult of Antonio's tasks, for he will spend several hours a day, working in the hot sun which brings the temperature above 100° F in the shade on hot afternoons. This heat is compounded by the heat of the boiling vat of water. Since handling the vat is a two-man job, Antonio needs assistance. His nephew helps him now, but when the nephew leaves to attend school, Antonio works out an agreement with one of the other men: You help me process my *yerba*, and when you are ready, I'll help you. This kind of working agreement is very common in wax camps.

The men begin their day's work at the vat by building a fire under it, using the dried, processed candelilla plant as fuel. Using a pitchfork, one of them must stoke the fire every five or ten minutes because the dried weed burns like tinder, though it produces a tremendous heat which will bring the vat of water to a boil in about thirty minutes. While one man is attending the fire, the other adds what water is necessary to bring the level to within about six inches of the top of the vat. He must also fill up a barrel with water to be used as needed throughout the day. All of this water is hauled in five-gallon buckets from the river. When the vat is filled with water, about a quart of sulfuric acid is added. This acid serves as a catalyst to help remove the wax from the outside of the plant. Antonio is no chemist and he doesn't understand how the acid works, but he knows that he gets more wax when he uses acid than when he doesn't.

Once the fire is started and the acid has been added, the two men fill the vat with the raw candelilla plant. Each bundle of *yerba* weighs about fifty pounds and the vat will hold about two bundles. In a good year when the plant yields much wax, the vat full of weed will produce about three or four pounds of wax.

When the vat is full of candelilla and tramped down by foot, the metal grate is placed on top of the vat and the weed is forced below the water level. As the water boils, the wax is melted from the weed and floats to the top as foam. Using the *espumador*, Antonio scoops the foam into a barrel placed at the end of the vat. Experience tells Antonio when it is no longer profitable to boil the weed further, since it is impossible to remove all of the wax from the plant. If an Anglo were processing the wax he would probably let his watch tell him how long to boil the weed, but Antonio lets experience guide him.

When this point is reached water is added to the vat to cool the contents and the fire is allowed to die down. The grate is removed and the weed is taken from the vat with pitchforks and stacked to dry, later to be used as fuel. The vat is again filled with raw candelilla plant, the fire is again stoked, and the process is repeated again and again until either there is no more plant to work with or until Antonio feels that it is time to quit work for the day.

As the wax in the barrel cools and hardens, the water goes to the bottom and is drained away. The wax is broken into small pieces and placed into a gunny sack. When Antonio finishes cooking all of his *yerba*, he takes his wax across the river and sells it. He can expect around seventy-seven cents a pound for it, but the market fluctuates. When he gets his money he returns to camp and repeats the cycle of gathering, processing and selling his wax.

When I first returned to a wax camp to study and observe, I had to squelch the urge to "improve" the modus operandi of the wax makers. In my infinite *gringo* superiority I thought that I could improve their methods. In the end, however, it was I who learned and they who taught.

Through tradition passed on by apprenticeship these Mexican wax makers have developed a system which is as effective as it will ever be. Normally we find that technology can increase output. But the candelilla wax processing along the border has not changed since the introduction of the steel vat in the 1920's or '30's. There is simply no more efficient way to gather the candelilla plant, transport it, and process it. Attempts to modernize have ended in dismal failure. A machine was designed by some enterprising *gringo* to harvest the plant by cutting and baling it. It worked in relatively flat areas, but was useless in the mountains where most of the weed grows. Besides, cutting the plant killed it, and re-planting became necessary. Attempts were made, again by enterprising *gringos* looking for a better way, to cultivate the plant by irrigating fields of candelilla. This failed because the plants would form little or no wax to protect the plant from moisture loss.

Burros are the most useful means of transportation in this mountainous region. They are cheap, they don't break down like a truck does, and if treated with any care at all they require no maintenance. In some areas trucks might be useful, but not in this rough terrain. Besides, machines tend to complicate matters for those who are not handy with machinery.

Various attempts have been made to improve the processing procedures to enable the Mexicans to recover more wax by making the vat a one-man job. This has been successful in the large villages and large stationary plants in the interior of Mexico, but not for this area, where mobility is necessary when the candelilla becomes scarce or when the *mordida* was not paid somewhere up the line and the *federales* come.

In observing these wax makers we note a fundamental difference between the way the Anglo approaches his work and the way Antonio approaches his. Antonio has learned to be comfortable with traditional ways. He is not inventive by Anglo standards; he does not attempt to build a better mouse trap, to devise a better way to extract the wax. He is willing to learn from tradition, to let it be his inventor. In some occupations the willingness to continue in the traditional methods has proved detrimental to progress, but among the candelilla wax makers along the Rio Grande, this dependence upon tradition has vindicated itself.

Candelilla plant

The vat is set into the riverbank with the firebox underneath.

Scooping the wax from the top of the vat with an *espumador*.

Antonio Avila taking a break.

Bundle of candelilla being loaded on a burro.

A bundle of candelilla tied the traditional way.

Cooking tortillas in camp.

A shelter typical of wax camps.

Burro loaded with candelilla and ready to return to camp.

Raw candelilla wax before it is delivered to the refinery.

The vat and raw candelilla.

GEOPHAGY IN THIS GENERATION

By Ava Bush

DURING the late winter and early spring of 1967, I observed an activity while traveling Highway 287, between Grapeland and Crockett (in Houston County) that left me wondering. People were digging into the roadside embankment. At first sighting I thought that they were looking for something lost, but as I continued to pass weekly, usually around four o'clock in the afternoon, the same scene was repeated, and always the people were Blacks. I learned later that they were digging clay to eat.

The next time I passed the clay bank I stopped and talked to a man and woman who were digging there. They were not anxious to talk about it, but they did say that they were collecting the hard dry lumps for the woman to eat. The man claimed he didn't eat clay.

I later dug some clay from the embankment and had it chemically analyzed. There was no mineral present in an amount sufficient to meet any human dietary deficiency. I tested clay from other areas of East Texas in order to compare physical and chemical properties and arrived at the same results. All of it was also rather flavorless. My interest in the subject increased when the school where I taught was integrated and two of my black female students told me that they were clay eaters.

Earth eating, or geophagy, is as old as man himself and records of its occurrence are found all over the world. The Persians were the first people known to follow the custom. Clay was available in Persian bazaars in two forms: hard white lumps from the Sumerian area and a grayish clay from the mountains of Malhallat. An analysis of fossilized human excreta, or coprolites, excavated near the city of Jarmo, Iraq, showed a high clay content, indicating that clay was a regular part of the people's diet.

Mythology and art remnants reveal that man's earliest practices of worship were linked with nature and clay eating. An omniscient snake god with the power to heal was worshiped in many parts of Asia Minor. The snake god, representing the male, ruled over the Earth Mother. In the worship of the Mother the soil itself became a ritualistic symbol, and the cultists ate the earth, which act, much like communion, orally incorporated the Mother into the worshiper and formed a mystical link between the participants and the goddess.

Geophagy as a primitive religious and ritualistic custom appears to have been a widespread phenomenon. Later it lost its religious significance and achieved success as an effective medicine. Egyptians were notable in their use of earth in its natural state for healing, and there are numerous references to the use of soil for both internal and external treatment. Even the gods of Egypt resorted to the use of earth for healing when necessary, although their divinity allowed them to add other ingredients to improve its taste. The Hebrews probably incorporated some of the Egyptian healing customs in their medical practices after their emigration from that country and their centuries-old bondage. Jesus used saliva mixed with earth when he healed the blind man.

The Greeks Hippocrates and Aristotle and the Romans knew the value of earth as a treatment for various complaints. The Chinese used clay for the treatment of dysentery; so did the Peruvians. Today, fine white china clay, known as kaolin, is incorporated into the medicine Kaopectate, found in every modern pharmacy, as one of the simplest and most effective remedies that we have for diarrhea. Clay, having absorptive properties, actually attracts and holds the disease-producing organisms.

Various culinary uses have also been found for earth. The Otomac Indians of South America use clay as a seasoning for their food, while the Indians of California added clay to their acorn bread to remove the tannic acid present. Cabeza de Vaca found friendly Texas Indians mixing earth with ground mesquite beans in order to sweeten the flavor. Navajos of New Mexico boiled their wild potatoes with clay to counteract the bad effects of excessive eating.

The modern custom of earth eating seems to exist as an end in itself rather than for culinary or medical reasons. The clay is not consumed as an additive or as part of a mixture, nor is it consumed in place of food. It is frequently eaten at the end of a meal as one would eat after-dinner mints or a dessert. Some of those who follow the practice, however, claim that they would gladly pass up a square meal in order to have a "bait" of clay. Distance or inaccessibility can always be overcome when a supply is needed.

The habit of clay eating often begins during a pregnancy when it is socially acceptable to have cravings. When this is the case the practice may be only temporary. Clay is eaten during pregnancy not only because of a strong desire for it but also for the beliefs that are associated with it. Some folklore has it that if a pregnant woman does *not* eat clay her baby will be marked by abnormal pigmentation patterns or with a distorted body. Belief also has it that clay eating during pregnancy promotes easy delivery by allowing the baby to "slide out." Midwives who deliver black babies declare that they can tell whether or not the mother ate clay during pregnancy by the appearance of the oily covering of the skin of the fetus. If she has been eating clay the oily covering is thick and flour like, sometimes showing scattered clay-like particles.

Without going into the psychological aspects of abnormal eating habits, clay eating does seem to be addictive. Medical records show that when confirmed clay eaters are hospitalized and subsequently deprived of their clay, they suffer all the withdrawal symptoms attributed to drugs, such as headache, nausea, insomnia, and rigors. In 1968 a thirty-five year old mother of six from Kilgore required extensive treatment in order to kick the habit, according to Dr. Murphy T. Scurry, who attended her at John Sealy Hospital.

Although many Blacks do their clay eating in secret and refuse to talk about it, most of them had no reservations and discussed it freely. Those East Texas Blacks interviewed ranged from teenagers to the elderly, both male and female, pregnant and fallow. The main reason given for eating clay was the simplest and most obvious: they liked the taste of it. They still like it even after they move north, and there is a steady flow of clay through the U.S. Mail from East Texas to Detroit and other points north. It will probably remain a popular but less familiar item of the soul food diet.

FIDDLERS AND FESTIVALS: A TEXAS TRADITION

By Joe Angle

Photographs by Kit van Cleave

E VERY YEAR in the small East Texas town of Crockett, fiddlers from around the state and the nation gather at the Davy Crockett Memorial Park, where the most skillful fiddler present is chosen. However, a description of this contest is incomplete if it stops with only the fiddler. For those attending the World's Champion Fiddlers' Contest, it is an annual custom and a social event of great significance.

On the northeast side of the semicircle of parked cars and pickups is located the pavilion, a large, tin-roofed shed under which the contest is held. Here people gather to hear the music they have grown up with, meet their friends, get in some gossip and judge the fiddlers. In front of the pavilion, under a large shade tree sits a wooden barrel full of water, with the name of the local funeral home printed on its side. On the south side are concession stands operated by the festival's sponsoring organization, Beta Sigma Phi. Also on this side is the registration table, shaded by a tent. A bit further east, is a group of chairs in which the contestants sit to await their chance at the prize money.

About seventy-five yards to the east of this area is a row of trees that follows the winding road through the park. Under the shade of these trees cars have been parked, and around these cars groups of fiddlers and guitar players gather for impromptu jam sessions. About four or five fiddlers and a couple of guitar players usually make up one of these groups. They agree upon one song and play it in its traditional key. Each takes his turn and plays until he is finished with his version or until one of the others in the group takes up the lead. When each has had his turn, they stop and chat a while before beginning another song. This is not indigenous to Crockett because it happens at all fiddling contests. This gives the fiddler a chance to hear and size-up his

59

opponents and to try to judge what kind of day he will have. This idea of the "good day" is quite strong among the old-time fiddlers. There are so many fiddlers of near equal skill that this plays a prominent part among the contestants in justifying the choice of the winner.

These informal sessions also provide an opportunity to get in all the fiddle playing desired. If the fiddler relied solely on his performance, that would mean only about five minutes of playing time, and the fiddler came to play. But, perhaps the most important function of the session is that it is a chance for the fiddler to meet and visit with old friends. There is a strong spirit of camaraderie among fiddlers. A large percentage of them know each other. Since they share in a unique talent and make some of the other contests, like those at Gilmer, Hurst, Athens, Pasadena, or Yoakum, close relationships are usually cemented. A good example of this is a story related to the author by Roy Garner, a long-time master of ceremonies at the Crockett contest. Garner had taken a group of past champions to the San Antonio World's Fair to perform. Every night after their performance they would gather at their motel and play until the early hours of the morning. When the group broke up Sunday night Garner went back to Crockett, but E. J. Hopkins and some other fiddlers gathered again at the motel. They played until early Monday morning. Hopkins then drove from San Antonio to Houston to start work that same morning as a city policeman.

It is under these trees at Crockett that a picnic lunch is often taken from the trunk of a car or off the tailgate of a pickup. This is also the place where the observers and the participants partake of the beer that is theoretically forbidden. Most people sit under the pavilion, but a large number of them mill about over the grounds talking and listening to the groups of fiddlers. There are people sitting under trees, people at the concession stands, kids playing chase, and scattered about are occasional pallets on which perspiring children and adults are lying.

One does not dwell on this subject long until some intriguing questions are asked. Why the fiddle? Why *this* music? Why a contest? When these questions are answered a great deal can be learned not only about contests but also about the very music everyone has gathered to hear and play.

It is well known that the American South was settled primarily by immigrants from the British Isles and that Texas was peopled by their sons and daughters from Tennessee, Mississippi, Alabama, and Louisiana. However, of not such general knowledge is the kind of music these souls brought with them. Music can be an evanescent thing especially where it is not written and is passed down by aural tradition. This is especially so when its habitat is the rough-hewn society of pioneer America. But one of the beauties of tradition is that it usually changes slowly and provides the scholar with a model of what went before. There may be a few additions or deletions but it is basically the same animal it always was. This is the situation with the fiddle tunes that can now be readily heard in any local contest, especially since there is an emphasis on the preservation of the traditional form.

When the immigrants came they of course brought their music. Look at the titles: "Billy in the Lowground," "Durang's Hornpipe," "Paddy on the Turnpike." England, Scotland, and Ireland fairly fall in your lap. This is not to say that what we listen to today is nothing but a collection of seventeenth and eighteenth century European folk-tunes. Far from it. This music has been embellished and modified by the American experience, but the relatively isolated rural life led in the American South resulted in its music leading a sheltered life from influences which would result in gross change or abandonment of the musical genre.

A thumbnail survey of this music reveals that it is tied directly to the dances commonly found in the British Isles during the seventeenth and eighteenth centuries. The names of the dances still survive and are commonly used, names like jig from Ireland, schottische and strathspey from Scotland, and hornpipe from England. In fact, the familiar Virginia Reel is a direct descendant of an English country dance found around Lancaster known as the "Sir Roger deCoverly." Even closer to home, when the fundamentalists succeeded in branding dancing as a vice to be avoided the "Virginia Reel" became metamorphosed into the play party game "Weevily Wheat" or as it was sometimes known "Waverly Wheat." However, all that was done was that the fiddle was dropped and the music was sung by the participants. The fiddle was eliminated because it was considered an instrument of the Devil. In fact, it was commonly believed that one had to sell his soul to the Devil at a crossroads at midnight in order to learn to play the fiddle. This probably goes a long way in explaining such old sayings as "thick as fiddlers in Hell."

Over the years the British, Irish, and Scottish tunes were modified and many of the titles were forgotten or changed to reflect life as it was found in the New World. Also a myriad of new tunes which aped their European ancestors in form were made up and passed down through succeeding generations. The names these works carry reflect almost any aspect of the public or private life of its originator: "Cotton Patch," "Forked Deer," "Soppin' the Gravy." Some of the titles are quite enigmatic: "Black Crook," and "Tom and Jerry."

One rather odd influence on fiddle music has been that of the Negro. This resulted in the richness of syncopation as well as some of the more popular current tunes like "Bile Them Cabbage Down," and "Ida Red." It seems odd now, but in the nineteenth and early twentieth centuries in Texas the black fiddler was quite common. Governor James S. Hogg often used his faithful Bob to entertain on the fiddle at the governor's mansion. Also, it was the black fiddler Arnold Schultz that was an early influence on Blue Grass music performer Bill Monroe.

The violin was not only the traditional instrument of the English country dance but its ease in transport and construction (Some were made of gourds and cigar boxes.) made it readily adaptable to frontier existence and a convenient substitute for the bulky bagpipe. The bagpipe had the misfortune to be associated with the royalist cause during the American Revolution. When the Tories and their sympathizers left, for all practical purposes so did the bagpipe. Only its memory and a certain amount of ingrained influence remained. The result was a mocking of the sound of the bagpipe on the fiddle. Listen to the droning and skirling in the original "Bonaparte's Retreat," and bagpipe influence becomes readily apparent.

One of the most unique aspects of fiddle music is that there are distinct regional styles. There is the breakneck speed of the Southeastern fiddler with his emphasis on double stopping (playing two strings at once). There are the New Englanders with their somewhat slower tempo and preference for the staccato styled jig. And there is the Texas style which is the slowest. It is this style that one will hear at Crockett and any other of the several fiddling contests held throughout the state. This style is characterized not only by its relatively slow tempo (about 120 beats per minute) but also by the paucity of double stopping. Further, the tunes are rendered in a very ornate, almost baroque manner with maximum use made of grace notes, turns, and slurred notes often referred to as the "Texas Roll." One other distinguishing factor is the intricacy of the accompaniment. Rather than the straight three-chord accompaniment that usually backs up most styles, the Texas accompanists expand on the basic three-chord structure of a fiddle tune and augment it with an expanded number of chords that still fit within the chord progression. This style of accompaniment is called "sock guitar." Also, in Texas one often finds a piano used as a background accompaniment.

The remarkable thing about regional styles is that even with the standardizing influences of mass media and ease of travel they stubbornly continue to exist, perhaps for the three following reasons. The first is family influence, secondly is the regional nature of the contest, and thirdly the influence of what I shall call the "patron saint."

There is a strong family influence among fiddlers. Fiddling is an aural art form since few fiddlers can even read music and therefore one that usually requires close tutelage. It is for this reason that the family unit lends itself so easily as a spawning ground for the new fiddlers. Fathers teach sons and sons teach their sons. This becomes readily apparent when the family histories of the fiddlers are explored. The important aspect of this is that basically the same style is taught.

Also the modern contest serves as a ground for the retrenchment of style. Aside from the fellowship involved, this is also a learning experience in which the fiddler either consciously or subconsciously picks up the style and musical passages of his friends. He then either modifies them or incorporates them *in toto* into his repertoire. In earlier days, styles were even more localized than now because of the difficulty of transportation. Transportation became easier and resulted in the expansion of the "locality." Forty years ago, convenient travel in rural Texas was pretty much limited to a few surrounding counties. Now, convenient travel has expanded and instead of surrounding counties, the modern fiddler finds it relatively effortless to travel halfway across the state, but not across the nation. So, there is still local influence, but the "locality" is simply larger.

Lastly, in Texas there are a few men whom a large percentage of Texas fiddlers follow as the paragons of style and technique. These musicians set the standards that others follow, thus acting as another force that tends to solidify regional style. Two such fiddlers that readily come to mind are Eck Robertson and Benny Thomasson.

With the fiddle firmly ensconced on the rural scene in the United States it did not take long for someone to think of the idea of having a contest to see who was the best fiddler in the area. Frequently, they were quite informal and only concerned one community or one county. Often the fiddlers would gather simply to play for an ice cream social or a box supper. In Crockett there had been gatherings of fiddlers at the north end of town or at the home of fellow fiddlers before there was ever a contest.

The date and location of the first formal contest is in doubt. Both Texas and the southeastern United States claim that distinction. While no date can be agreed upon, most people put around the turn of the century. One contest, the annual Atlanta, Georgia, Old Fiddlers' Convention, began as early as the 1880's. By the 1920's notices began to appear in newspapers but the contests remained localized because of the difficulty and expense of travel.

The guiding light for the Crockett Fiddlers' Festival was V. B. Tunstall, Sr., known in the area simply as "Barker." He made his living by teaching music, doing some barbering, and tuning pianos. While he went about his work he carried his violin, and when he got the chance he would have a fiddling session with one of his customers or with one of the families whose piano he had tuned. It was this man who was to lead in the establishment of an annual event that has lasted more than thirty-five years, Crockett's World's Champion Fiddlers' Festival. In fact, his name became so closely connected with the contest that it was often referred to as "Barker Tunstall's Old Fiddlers' Festival," and after he died succeeding contests were dedicated to his memory.

One day in 1937, Tunstall, along with Terry Van Pelt, Raymond Cornelius. W. E. Keeland, and Homer Galloway gathered in Cornelius's hotel. They believed that the old fiddle tunes were in danger of becoming extinct, so they made preliminary plans for a fiddlers' festival to be held in Crockett. However, the festival was to be more than simply a plan for preservation. It was to be a day of fun for those who listened as well as those who played. The men formed committees which took care of the arrangements of publicity, fund raising, and the securing of facilities. The committee's personnel changed from time to time until the late 1940's when the festival was taken over by the local Jaycees.

The publicity, such as there was, was handled by Tunstall. During the course of his years in the music business he had come to know quite a number of fiddlers in the area. In order to spread the word, he began writing the fiddlers he knew, telling them of the new contest. As things progressed and the operation of the contest changed hands, letters were still sent out and notices appeared in local newspapers. Tunstall began to publish poems with fiddling and contest themes in the local newspaper.

The money for the prizes came from the donations made by local merchants. At first, the prizes were meager, no doubt reflecting the hard times of the 'thirties. The top prizes were $50 and $25. Lesser prizes were various types of goods such as groceries and boxes of cigars. Later the "kind" was dropped and only cash prizes were given, with the prize money reaching several hundreds of dollars.

Mr. Tunstall also arranged for the judges, who usually came from surrounding towns. In the early days of the festival the fiddlers were judged on the tune, *i.e.*, its difficulty and the manner in which it was played, harmony (the harmony produced by double stopping, or bowing two strings at once), and audience reception. This applied to both the individual fiddler and the band. It soon became evident that this method led to the winner being determined almost solely by audience appeal. So in 1954 this was changed and for a number of years the contest was conducted on a kind of double standard. There was one set of standards for the individual fiddler and one set (the old set) for the fiddle bands. Things continued in this light until 1961 when the fiddle band contest was dropped.

The new manner of judging starts off by giving every fiddler twenty-five points in each of four categories: tune, timing, bowing, and fingering. From this the judges begin to deduct points for mistakes they observe. The bow must be held correctly and be properly titled, and the little finger must be kept folded in. If the little finger sticks out, it is called "letting the finger sail or fly." Notes must be made with the proper finger and the bottom of the hand must be kept off the neck of the violin. The tune must be played in its original key and be of some degree of difficulty, and the tempo must be steady. The three judges sit in the audience with a score sheet and observe and listen to each fiddler. They then tally up his score.

The judges for the fiddlers' festival go through a screening period of about three years. Their competence in playing the fiddle is determined; the opinion of others as to their honesty is checked, and their conduct at other contests is observed. The individual is then put on a waiting list to await his chance at being a judge. This is quite different from the days when Barker Tunstall would simply pick the judges for the contest from among his acquaintances.

The contest is divided into three age categories: seventy-five years and up, fifty to seventy-five, and fifty and under (one year there was a twenty and under group). Each group plays separately, with each fiddler playing two songs, aided by one accompanist. The songs that are played must be traditional (a very elastic term) and there must be no singing or trick fiddling, *i.e.*, playing the fiddle behind the back or between the legs. A first, second, and third place winner for each category is chosen. There is then a play-off between these nine contestants to determine the winner of the festival. The winner of the festival then meets the previous World's Champion to determine the World's Champion for that year. At this step, each play-off contestant must play a breakdown, a rag, a polka, a waltz, and a tune of his choice. The World's Champion, besides getting prize money, has his name engraved on the large festival trophy, and he keeps a "traveling" trophy until the next year when he returns to defend his title. If he wins three times in a row, he keeps the traveling trophy and is retired from competition.

In the beginning, the contest was held on the east side of the courthouse which occupied the town square. The program began about 10:00 a.m. At this time the stage was left open to anyone who wishes to perform. At noon the fiddlers were given a barbecue dinner in the space behind the local hotel. After World War II the festival was moved to the city park, much to the delight of the local businessmen who found that having it on the square caused a hopeless traffic snarl. The contest was held on the west side of the park with the fiddlers performing on a raised open platform. The platform still stands but is not used because as the festival began to grow it became necessary in 1955 to build the pavilion now in use.

After the first year the state prison system has always sent a musical group to provide entertainment. Two of the more popular groups were the Goree Girls from the Goree Farm and the Eastham Farm Prison Swingsters. It is not really clear whether it is their talent or the fact that they are prisoners that accounts for their popularity. I remember one prisoner who made a great success out of his appearance by singing a song called "Please Release Me."

The "outside" entertainment, however, has included more than what the prison system provides. Usually, the appearance of some well known country-and-western performer or group is arranged for the dance that follows the contest. A great favorite in the early years was the Lightcrust Doughboys who provided the music for the gubernatorial campaign of "Please Pass the Biscuits Pappy" W. Lee O'Daniel. Crockett and Houston County were carried handily by O'Daniel which perhaps goes a long way in explaining the group's popularity.

The more popular the professional entertainment, the more attendance at the dance. This is most important to the festival. The proceeds from the dance go to help defray the costs of the festival, and while the day is devoted to the fiddler, the dance is pushed for this reason. A good example is the crowd that attended in 1954 which was one of the largest. That year the featured attraction was Bob Wills and the Texas Playboys. Wills is best known as the pioneer of western swing that was quite popular during the late 'thirties and 'forties as well as the artist who recorded "San Antonio Rose."

There have been other attractions at the festival beside the fiddlers and recording stars. For a few days the cowboy film personality "Monty" Montana Hale made appearances to dutifully sign autographs and give shooting demonstrations. Square dancing and square-dance calling contests were also held. There have also been visits by the Alabama-Coushatta Indians. They entertained the crowds with their dancing and by just generally being Indians. In the late 1940's and early 1950's a beauty contest was conducted and girls from Crockett and the surrounding communities between the ages of sixteen and twenty vied for the honor of being queen of the festival. During the Davy Crockett craze of the 1950's a contest for boys under thirteen years was sponsored by a surgical dressing company in conjunction with the introduction of their new "Davy Crockett First Aid Kit." In 1961 and 1962 there were fly-ins to the Houston County Airport. A complimentary breakfast and transportation to the festival were provided for the participants by the Crockett Community Council.

If all this sounds corny and provincial, the people of Houston County could not care less. It is their festival and they will schedule and provide the things that lie within their resources and tastes. They are not accountable to anyone else for their likes and dislikes. The music they gather to listen to represents for many a pleasant relief from the sounds of mass man and his mass culture. For some, it is a symbol of rebellion against the age, a symbol of individualism. But it is not the root-less and anarchic individualism so much in vogue, for it has not di-vorced itself from its past. It stands healthily within the traditions of the area. For others the music is simply a part of life. They are the dif-ference between "being" and "observing."

Manifestations of an "agrarian myth?" Maybe. But even if it is, there is a certain amount of value and truth to some myths, and what-ever this myth's qualities are, it is certainly one that is believed by a great number of people. For proof all one has to do is tune to a coun-try-and-western radio station and count the songs which for all prac-tical purposes sing the praises (both real and imagined) of life in the country. The modern fiddle contest has its message. It is an on-going link between the present and the past.

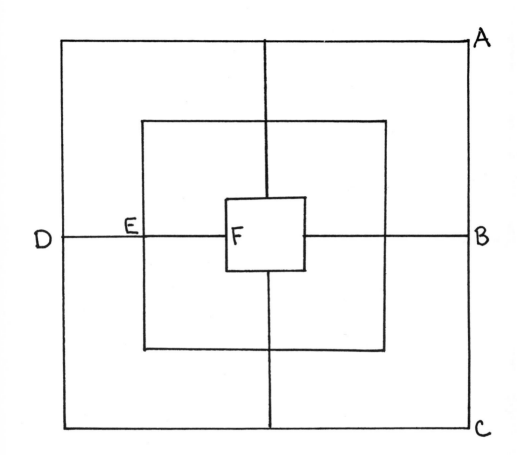

A LESSON ON PLAYING MUHLE

By Leon Hale

At WINEDALE, the Germany-flavored rural community in Fayette County near Round Top, I stopped in at Wagner's store and got Lee Wagner to give me a lesson on how to play Muhle. Muhle is the German noun for mill, a machine for grinding grain. It's also the name of an old beer-drinking game that immigrated to Texas from Europe long ago when German settlers came here. Wagner says just the old timers play it now around Winedale. It's a good example of a folk game once popular in parts of Texas where the German influence is strong.

Muhle is played, like most folk games, with whatever materials are handy around a home or farm or local gathering place. First you need a diagram, or a board, which you can draw with any kind of marker. Sometimes you find Muhle boards chalked on the bars of country taverns. Wagner showed me how to draw one to go with this Muhle report.

At first the game seems to be a combination of checkers and tick-tack-toe. But it gets pretty complex. Toward the end it takes on some of the characteristics of chess. Two play the game. They begin with an equal number of men, or pieces. Say nine pieces each. The pieces can be buttons—white for you, black for me. Or they can be corn kernels—yellow for you, white (or red) for me. I wonder if this use of corn isn't a clue as to the origin of the game's name. You take turns placing buttons on the board. They may be placed anywhere there's a corner or an intersection, and they may also be moved, one space at a time. The object is to get three buttons in a row. Then you've "made a mill," and captured one of your opponent's buttons.

Take a look at the drawing. A mill could be made, for example, by placing buttons at Points A, B, and C. Also at Points D, E, and F. Your buttons must be lined up at consecutive points. What I mean, you couldn't make a mill with buttons at D, F, and B. When a player is reduced to only three buttons left on the board, he is given a defensive advantage. That is, he can jump those three buttons anywhere on the board, to block his opponent. That's when the game gets pretty deep, and you see a lot of head-scratching. You've lost the contest when your opponent leaves you with only two buttons. No way you can make a mill, with just two. There are other refinements to this game I haven't got room to tell you about.

Wagner's daughter-in-law Marilyn was in the store and the two of them played another old German game, with one die (half of a pair of dice, I mean) and a homemade board that looks something like a Monopoly setup. You toss the die and the number of spots that comes up determines how many spaces around the board you can move your button. The most interesting thing to me about this game is its name. Wagner wrote it down for me as he thought it would read in German— *Mench Arger Dicht Nich*. He said that would translate in a loose way to "Friend, don't get upset." The name comes from a situation a player faces in the game, when he's about to win and one toss of the die can send him back to the beginning to start all over.

While I was at Winedale I met Delphine Hinze and he told me about some of the German outdoor games he used to play when he was a boy. One is Sautreiben, which means sow-driving. In this one a circle of players (any number) is equipped with sticks and they're defending a hole in the center of the circle. The sow driver, or the man who's "it," tries to drive the "sow," a rubber ball, through the defenders and put it in the hole in the ring. Action gets pretty wild. Sautreiben is not played much any longer because it's apt to produce too many busted shins and skulls from all those heavy sticks flailing away in a crowd.

I think I'd prefer the indoor game of Muhle, if I could get good at it. My first game Lee Wagner needed only about five minutes to take all my buttons away from me.

CHIMNEY DOBBIN' IN THE BIG THICKET

By Cecil V. Overstreet

Photographs from the
Larry Jene Fisher Collection,
Lamar University Library

THE REASON that people in the Big Thicket built stick-and-dirt chimneys was that there was nothing else to build them out of. Stones would have to be cut and hauled in, but dirt was plentiful and near at hand. These old chimneys and fireplaces were built to provide heat for the house. They were also the place where the food was cooked in most of the early homes. Not many people had or could afford a stove, even if they were available, and in most communities they were not.

The usual fireplace room, or living room, had a fireplace that was used for warming mostly and was built level with the floor. I can very well remember many houses that had dirt floors. They were made of the same type of dirt that was used to construct the mud chimneys. They were made by packing the dirt on the floor until it was set up. That is, it was wet down and let dry with enough sand in it to cause it to set up hard. It was easy to keep clean with a broom made of sedge grass. These floors were very clean and neat, in most instances. After they had set they were very stable and could take a lot of abuse, and it took a lot of water to break them down. The board floors were split from logs and shaped with a broad-axe and were fairly level to walk on. There were always cracks in these puncheon floors but this proved useful too. Pet hogs had the habit of sleeping under the house during the winter time, if you didn't have a rail or picket fence to keep them out of the yard. At night they would get to "pulling cover" and squealing and grunting, and the only way you could run them out so you could sleep was to pour hot water on them through the cracks in the floor.

The other type of fireplace—the one to cook on—was made with a hearth that was raised eighteen or twenty inches above the floor level. It had a rack made of hardwood poles or an iron bar above the fire to hang the pots on. The baking was done with cast-iron Dutch ovens which had three legs to raise it up off the fire and a cupped lid to hold coals on top. This fireplace was in the kitchen, which was usually built apart from the living quarters and had a covered walk connecting it to the house. The kitchen was set apart from the main house because it presented a greater fire hazard.

Chimneys and furnaces for syrup cookers and hog scalders were also built out of sticks and mud. The syrup kettle was set up over a furnace with a fire box in it. The fire door was in one end and the chimney was at the other. This pulled the fire across and under the kettle, keeping it uniformly hot, while putting the smoke up in the air so the syrup makers could work better and not be smothered by the smoke and fire.

The hog scalding kettles were set up in much the same way and made butchering much faster and easier and for the same reasons. Every family in the Thicket had woods hogs on the open range that they worked and marked just the same as cattle. The hogs got fat on the mast —the acorns, beech nuts, and pecans—in the winter and were then killed and cured. Most families got enough lard and meat from their hogs to last until the following winter. They also had cows that they ate fresh in the summer. Much of the beef, however, was dried, or tassoed, over a smoke and seasoned with lots of salt and red pepper to keep the skippers from getting in it. This meat along with a plentiful supply of wild game gave the kitchen fireplace plenty to work on.

When a house was built, in most instances the chimney was built on the north end of the house so the heat would drift back into the room during the cold winter weather which blew in from the north. In the summer the wind, mostly from the south, caused the heat to leave the house faster, thus making it more comfortable when cooking on a fireplace. The trouble with this location of the chimney was that the north wind which blew in the winter when you were trying to keep warm with the biggest fires caused the sparks to blow over the roof, increasing the fire danger.

The chimney was begun after the house was almost completed. At that time the opening for the fireplace was cut in the wall, and after the chimney was all the way up, the roof was finished around all but the outer side of it. The roof was fitted close to the chimney to prevent the chimney from washing away during a heavy rain.

The chimney was framed by putting up four tall posts, usually hewn from rich-lighter pine or from long-straw or rosemary pine, which were straight and didn't taper much, I'd say less than two inches in ten feet. The frame poles tapered from about six inches at the bottom to four inches at the top. They were squared off with a broad-axe on the sides where the cross pieces were to be nailed. The cross sticks were split out of pine also. They were nailed, pegged, or just stacked one over the other as the mud of the chimney went up. It was necessary that at least some of them be fastened to the chimney posts to hold the posts in position until the mud dried, after which the structure would stand by itself.

Some chimneys were framed by boring holes in the risers, then joining them with rounded sticks. This type of frame had to be completed before it was raised, and the sticks had to be in place before the mud was put on any of them.

When everything else was ready the mud had to be gotten for "the chimney dobbin'." This was usually what we call mayhaw pond mud. Mayhaws grow naturally in a wet heavy soil that has enough clay to cause it to be sticky and hold its shape when wet, and it has enough sand in it to set up hard enough to keep from getting washed away by the rain. You also had to have a binder, something to hold the dirt together until it set up. This was usually Spanish moss but it could be pine straw or plain grass hay. The dirt was hauled in on a ground sled if it was close or in a wagon if there was a long way to go.

Before the chimney—or the house, for that matter—could be built there had to be a water supply. During the settling of the Big Thicket the underground water level was from ten to twenty feet. You could dig a water well anywhere in this area in quick order. I saw Mr. Tom Laird and his oldest son Albert dig a well in one day that supplied water for at least thirty head of mules used to log with. They began in the morning when we went into the woods to work, and that evening at quitting time there was already plenty of water in the mule troughs, drawn from the well with buckets and a rope. The water level has dropped in the Thicket around a foot each year for the last twenty years.

A hole was dug in the ground, or a box with pole sides was built to mix the mud in. Then the dry dirt and binder was dumped in the pen and water was added to get it to the right consistency. The mixers got barefooted and stomped around in the mud to mix it. Sometimes the binder was added later, the mixers working the moss into one "cat" or mud ball at a time as they made it. The mud was then worked onto the chimney sticks which were framed around the risers one after the other until the chimney was topped out, eighteen inches or two feet above the comb of the house. The daubers shaped the mud by hand as they went along, forming it into about equal thickness on the four sides of the frame. They covered the sticks and risers so they could not be reached by flame after the chimney was put in use. The back side of the chimney was about six inches from the cabin's inside wall as another protection against fire.

The base of the chimney was made from mud without binder up to the level of the fireplace, which usually extended out from the inside wall at least a foot. The hearth was shaped to the owner's fancy. In my time most of them had an arched hearth, the arch being made from a worn-out crosscut saw. All the hearth work was framed the same as the chimney, with short posts and sticks that reached along the sides and all the way from the chimney posts to the inside face of the structure. The hearth fronts were smoothed out real clean and dried out a dull white and were real hard.

These old hearth and chimneys lasted for years and were easily repaired. If a chunk fell off anywhere all you had to do was to get some mud and replace it. This was a part of getting ready for winter.

This chimney is being built at Virgil Rosier's log house near Thicket, Texas, in the 1920's. The workers are Clint Cooper and Virgil Rosier on the scaffold and J. E. Rosier and Bill Smith on the ground.

Forming the mud into a "cat." It has already been mixed by tromping.

Tossing a "cat" to a dauber.

Daubing the chimney.

Nailing on another stick.

Daubing the chimney.

The chimney reaches the eaves where the flashing is worked in.

Topping the chimney out at sundown.

JINKINS SEED STORE, NACOGDOCHES

By Tim Van Riper

CEDARCUTTERS AND OTHERS

By C. W. Wimberley

THE CEDARCUTTER'S ancestor was among the poor-white pioneer stock who came to take up land, to carve their small places among the hills, and to hang onto the stubborn soil by their teeth and fierce pride. Restless in spirit, he revolted against the slow ways of the plow or following the herds and in time found his ties to the land with his ax and the cedars. The clan was born of his breed. From woodchopper, railcutter, and charcoal burner to cedarcutter was but a small step, once barbed wire created the market for his post.

The cedarcutter was among the last of the truly independent American craftsmen and cutting posts was his chosen trade. He possessed a special skill with the ax which he used to turn cedar timber into the most marketable kind of post with the least expense of time and effort. His day's work was done within a matter of four or five hours, and during that time he could produce upwards to a hundred good clean-cut post if he were working in fair timber. Though he always worked standing on another person's property, he lived and passed into oblivion without having ever known the feel of wearing another man's collar—union or boss.

The cedarchopper was a lesser member of the tribe. Though he might be able to chop several cords of oak firewood in a day, he was never quite able to master the cedarcutter's special skill with the little double-bit cedar ax. Any day he produced a hundred good posts, he accomplished the feat by ample use of brute strength and endurance. His ties to the cedarbrakes were loose.

The cedarwhacker was a reckless, careless rogue. He didn't give a damn. Using any sort of an old ax, he would tackle his job with wild abandon. He could turn good timber into the sorriest looking post, leave a sloven mess where he made a track, give you the shirt off his back while stealing you blind, have you laughing ten minutes after you had hunted him down to break his damned neck, never around when you needed him, and about the time you got around to thanking your Lord for good riddance of the pest, he'd show up again grinning from ear to ear.

The cedarwhacker took to the cedars like a blind beaver with the hiccups but with less favorable results. The pitiful post he produced spelled starvation. Either he developed some skill with the ax in a hurry or turned to brush cutting or became some cedarchopper's grunt. The cedarbrakes held no promise for him.

Traveling in the mode of itinerant farmers or squatters in search of new land, cedarcutters had not severed all ties to their pioneer stock. They rode on wagons drawn by willow-tailed ponies, heaped high with their plunder, and topped with ragged children and coops of chickens. Hidden somewhere among the cracked dishes and dirty bedding, there were packets of seeds and roots of vegetables and flowering plants growing in cans, and hounds or feists or cur breeds trotting alongside, and a milk cow tethered behind and bringing up the rear. Sometimes there was also a donkey or little mule that had been trained to drag logs and poles through brush from deep canyons.

At camp sites near water they stopped to throw up their rag houses or shanties of tin and scrap lumber and brush—to chop select timber into post so long as the brake suited their whim—to follow hounds at night—to dance barefoot to fiddles on grounds cleared among the cedars—to curse and fight and drink raw whiskey—to take their women and raise their children—all done in strange ways foreign to other eyes.

Though the timber belonged to the cedarman, the cedarcutter chopped for himself. The post he cut belonged to him until they had been hauled to the yard, checked, entered into ledgers, and he had been paid his full fair share of their value. He was his own man with his earnings determined only by his skill and effort.

The cedarman could determine the grade and price he would receive for his post, and the brake boss could set rules for running the brake, but nobody, nobody, could tell the cedarcutter anything he had to do. No anchors held him in place and he drifted with the first restless wind. He was among the last of an independent breed.

In his time, Snuffy Pruett was a real cedarcutter from the old school. One day his old truck groaned onto the cedaryard under a load of post that made everybody set up and take notice. Before Snuffy's kids perched on the load had time to climb down, the cedarchecker was a-blowing about the size of this load, how good a grade the post was and how nice they were trimmed—like Snuffy had always done. Even the cedarman got into the show by saying Snuffy's bunch was about the best danged cedarcutters he'd ever had, and everybody around had something good to say about Snuffy that day.

With his chest swelling out bigger and bigger every minute, Snuffy says we hadn't seen nothing yet. He knew where there was many another load of post better than them in that brake and he was going to get ever last one of them. He liked this place and everybody around. He had found the pie in the sky and contentment was his.

The cedarman gave Snuffy a swig from his bottle in private and Snuffy demanded everybody have a soda water with him at the commissary store before he headed for his camp.

About twelve o'clock that night the dogs began to bark and set up a howl along Honey Creek. Also, if you had listened closely you could hear chickens and kids squalling over toward Snuffy's camp site. Around two a.m. Snuffy fired up his old truck and you wondered why in the devil a man would be going to town at this hour.

The next morning, Snuffy's camp site stood as empty as a last year's bird nest. Kids, dogs, cats, chickens, raghouse, washtubs, the pepper plants growing in cans—everything was gone.

The cedarman wanted to know why? The puzzled cedarchecker stood fingering his chin while the cedarhands anxiously offered all sorts of speculations.

If one had been included, any old cedarcutter could have told them the event was no riddle. "Hell, a man's got the rights to his own mind without havin' to have a reason. Ain't he? He jest went on; that's all there is to it. Nothin' else."

Honest John was another one of the great cedarcutters during the Depression. In the cool of early morning, John's cedar wagon would take off for the brake with kids in and on and hanging all over this Model-A Ford Tudor Sedan. With a wife who could swing a pretty wicked ax and a bunch of kids who cut their eye-teeth on ax handles, this tribe could stump a jag of cedar posts about as quick as you could shuck and shell a peck of ear corn. By nine-thirty or ten o'clock, a couple of the younger boys would pull on to the cedaryard with piles of poles riding the front fenders, post sticking from both back windows and a four-foot stack racked a-top the rear bumper. Sometimes they would make the second or third of such loads before the Tudor came in on its final run for the day with kids and cedar posts in and all over it and John's head hanging out to see where he was headed.

Usually there was an armadillo or two lying on the floorboards of the last load. John's wife could grind off a batch of armadillo sausage that tasted, looked like, and ate as good as Mr. Anybody's pork and, if you paid no heed to bone structure, her armadillo shank fried in deep fat surpassed most pig.

Disaster never seemed to strike these people; they lived with it. One time John was traveling along with his load of kids and cedar when a blow-out spat a home-made boot as big as a man's hat from a front tire, sending the Ford Tudor on a swerving course across the ditch to break a rural telephone pole off at the ground and knock three big posts from a rancher's fence. No blood was shed, no cussing hard luck was spilled, and extra dips from the bottle of snuff sufficed. John left the scene with three green stays baling-wired in to hold the fence in place, the phone lines sagging in the air, and his load topped with three new, dry, heart-post and a ten-foot pole—all barked, butted a-new, and freshly blazed.

This era—from before the turn of the century through the Depression—was the heyday of the cedar business in Texas. Fortunes were made and lost by the cedarmen, the yard operators. The virgin cedar-brakes of heart timber stood much as they had during the Indian days, and timber rights to large tracts of land could be bought for a song. No clearing of brush was involved in these deals, they just harvested the post as they pleased. Within a twenty-year span, the cedars had grown a new crop of four-inch posts; therefore, these old brakes could be reworked again and again, maybe cutting the timber a bit closer with each new operation. Also, with the tall grasses gone the way of the buffalo, new brakes were being grown as the cedars spread to cover new areas of overgrazed lands.

The cedar kings ran a loose herd, for judged by any time standards, it was a bastard business they operated. Each cedarman ran his own show in his own way and none was ever quite able to put his collar on the cedarcutter tribe, no matter what his methods. Any cagey move and hell broke loose and his business could go up in smoke. The successful cedarmen, the cedar kings, were characters worthy of their day. Had to be.

During this period, Homer Rogers operated yards along the Nueces River. To tie his operation to the railhead at Campwood, he built a narrow-gauge railroad up the river. The track was laid on hewn cedar crossties which, after the project had been abandoned, were sold to be used as fence post in a wide area of Texas. Some of these crossties are still standing in fences on Llano County ranches.

Old Sholton—a name I use here because the oldtimers did differ in the spelling and the initials they gave—operated his businesses in the Falls Creek area with yards in the brakes and at Tow Valley (now headwaters of Lake Buchanan on the Colorado River). The railhead and shipping point was located downstream at Kingsland. With a Prussian methodical approach to all matters, he tried to eliminate hauling the post by wagon from the cedaryards to the railhead.

This first try was an elaborate fiasco. Determined to float his post as rafts down the Colorado, he built large booms to fish these rafts from the river near the railroad. While the river ran low, he had the rafts assembled along the banks of the Colorado near old Tow Valley and awaited a freshet. The freshet came and the rafts were on their way. But the old Colorado was a wild and untamed river in those days. The freshet was merely the quiet forerunner to the rip snorting torrents of a flood. The rafts passed Kingsland like the highball express and scattered Sholton's post down the Colorado watercourse to the Gulf of Mexico.

Smitten but undaunted, Sholton had to have another try. This time, a steam tractor was used to draw six floats loaded with post, traveling a new route from Tow Valley to the Iron Spur, a railroad siding between Kingsland and Llano. To replenish the tractor's water supply, wells were drilled along the way. One of these wells is still in use today at the Hodge Nobles place and another at the Hudson Hereford place.

Another fiasco was in the making. The tractor's iron wheels spun on rocks and mired in mud and the devil was to be paid all along the way. On top of all that, the limestone in the water soon clogged the tractor's boiler tubes and another effort went down the drain. So, Buck Nobles, one of the haulers, was still in business. Using a little span of hard-tailed mules hitched to his farm wagon, Buck made two round trips per day, earning two dollars and fifty cents each trip. Five dollars was a real good day's wages for a man and his team to make in them good old days.

This last story doesn't have much to do with cedar cutting, but it's about one of the real old-time cedarcutters.

Flatnose Joe earned his moniker early in his career by arguing with one of the Young boys about the grade of a post.

With the post held in one hand and the four-inch horseshoe measure in the other, Joe was demonstrating that the top end of the post could easily be passed between the prongs of the horseshoe without the bark touching either side, and it damn well wasn't a four-inch post.

Meanwhile, without a word Young had eased one of the wagon standards out of its loops and settled the argument with one wild swing that left Joe flat on his back. The Youngs were like that and Joe's nose was never the same.

In addition to the flat nose, the wagon standard must have also given Joe a split personality. While he was Joe, he was a cedarcutting dude. But, when old Flatnose came to the surface, he was like a house cat on the kitchen table. If his head wasn't hung in the cream pitcher, he was sniffing at the butter bowl or lapping at the gravy dish.

During the early 'twenties, Pfieffer ran a cedaryard in old Tow Valley and Joe was around to give the camp life some color. He was married then and old enough to have some sense, but wife and time had not slowed down Joe's roving eye.

One night, with a lantern held in one hand and the other concealed beneath her apron, Joe's wife prowled the camp hunting for her husband. At the far side of the camp she burst into a stranger's tent to hold her lantern above a bed where Joe lay beside another cedarcutter's woman. Lowering the lantern, she brought the other hand from under the apron to point the barrel of Joe's pearl-handled six-shooter right between the other woman's eyes. She then began a tirade which berated this wench below the level of being worth the price of the powder and lead; otherwise, she would pull the trigger.

While these words flew, Joe slipped his feet from inside the covers into his boots, grabbed his pants and hat, and made a run for it, clad only in his long johns.

As he cleared the tent flaps, his wife got off a couple of shots that were close enough for Joe to know that this time, the old gal meant business. This was not going to be one of those rabbit runs of zigging and zagging and sweet talking. Adding distance between him and the lantern he set a course across the old Thorpe place towards the cedars. And found his Waterloo.

The Thorpes had drawn their water from a hand-dug well, four feet in diameter and some twenty-odd feet deep. Several pieces of old lumber laid across this well had prevented any cattle from falling into it. Under Joe's weight they crumbled. With a splash he stood trapped neck deep in water, and the lantern soon dangled overhead.

Joe's best honied words were wasted as his wife cleared away the remaining lumber, lay flat on her stomach, lowered the lantern, and took a steady aim with the pearl-handled sixshooter.

About the time the sixshooter barrel steadied, Joe's head ducked beneath the water. When he could no longer hold his breath his head surfaced near the side of the well. As the barrel steadied again, down he'd go again. With little room to maneuver and that sixshooter barrel staring him in the eye every time he looked up, Joe was soon winded. With a final half-hearted plunge, he came up gasping, "My God, woman, hurry up and shoot. Can't you see I'm running out of breath?"

Where's Joe's finest words had failed, his anguish struck a different chord. His wife began to laugh, and the more she looked the more she laughed. And laughing she finally left the scene.

Sometime later she did tell some of the hands that her husband had fallen into a well and where he might be found, if they had nothing better to do.

A way of life is gone from the Texas cedarbrakes and the hills are not the same. Born hard to die hard, the cedarcutter belongs to the past. Descendant of a tribe spawned during the dying days of the Old West, he now stands a stranger among the people on his native soil, on land the Indian's peaceful splinter tribes were ground into oblivion by the cedarcutter's ancestors. Then he too found his fate. For just as the sands of time have claimed the final fragments of many cultures in the ancient past, today the remnants of his tribe are being worn away—marked only by man's indifference to his own kind.

FIRST MONDAY AT CANTON AND SOME TALES THEY TELL

By Jim Harris

Photographs by Robert Morris Abernethy

G. K. CHESTERTON once wrote about a place in London where fake poets lived, a place that did not produce poetry but that was itself a poem. Sometimes I think of Canton, Texas, like that. Clear out all the fake antique dealers from Dallas who crowd into the place on First Monday weekend, and what's left is a place that does not produce poetry but that is a poem. Clear out the folks who travel once a month, and what's left is a collection of traveling poems seen throughout the Southwest—a fifty-year-old ex-champion bull rider looking for a rodeo, or an old farmer in the '59 pickup full of hunting dogs.

Go over to the east side of town, along Mill Creek, on Saturday night, and get drunk with their dogs, or their food, or their stories.

The traders of dogs and horses and goats, of plates and jars and lamps, or harnesses and tools and anvils, have been coming to Canton on the first Monday of each month for a long time. (Actually people trade on Monday and the weekend before.) Legend has it that the first First Monday took place before the Civil War and a Centennial was celebrated in 1973. How it got started is anyone's guess.

The realists believe Canton settlers from Alabama and Tennessee continued a tradition started in their home states. The romantic folk believe First Monday originated with imaginative early settlers who liked to visit with neighbors once a month. Probably, the truth lies between the two extremes. Definitely, the origin had something to do with the fact that county court convened in Canton the first Monday of each month. (W. S. Mills has more of the stories about the origin of First Monday in his *History of Van Zandt County*.)

Through the years trades day in Canton changed from a disorganized gathering to a meticulously planned affair, thanks to the awakening of the townspeople to the economic possibilities of the occasion. At first, mules and horses were sold and traded, prompting some to call it "Hoss Monday." At other times other commodities dominated the trading. For instance, hogs became the important medium of exchange for awhile. Another time more dogs were bartered than anything else; this caused people to call the gathering "Dog Monday." Today, just about anything can be found on the grounds during First Monday weekend. Due in part to a national craze for things old, First Monday seems to have moved into an antique phase, and truck· loads of ancient guns, or furniture, or bottles are bought and sold.

One item can be had for free. Tales of Canton, of the origin of trades day, and of big swaps can be had for the asking. Up around the square or down on the trading grounds, people talk and relate the lore associated with First Monday.

In fact, people tell stories whether asked or not. Over the years the narrating of First Monday tales has become a custom that reinforces the narrator's importance in the festive group and gives the individual a sense of identity with a group that includes Red River poor and Fort Worth rich. That is, the telling of First Monday tales is a custom within a larger custom, the monthly celebration for trade and talk. In this sense it should not be separated from the larger custom because it functions to promote and propagate the larger event. In another sense it should be dealt with as a separate custom. Telling stories about the trading days satisfies personal needs as well as group needs. The variety of personal needs can be seen in at least three large groups of storytellers: the "down-home dealers," the townspeople, and the "uptown dealers."

The down-home dealers seem most anxious to relate stories. For them, the custom brings "back-home" to Canton and serves less to promote a sale than to satisfy some personal need to talk. Many of the stories I heard the dog traders tell fall into this category. A man may tell of a great hunt to brag or simply for the joy of telling the narrative. Around the campfires on Friday and Saturday nights men tell stories with no intention of selling or trading.

The townspeople, those who live in Canton all month, seem more conscious of promotion. Up in the barber shop, or across from it on the oldtimer's benches, the story impulse seems always to be checked by the impulse to promote good business. This is not to say their stories are inferior. Some of the best trading stories I heard came from the men in the barber shop and on the square.

For a third group of tellers, those I am calling the "uptown dealers," promotion appears the dominant impulse. Good stories come from them, too, but they are more polished, tend to impress the listener rather than entrap him. Many of the spaces are rented to businesses from the surrounding cities, Dallas to the east, Tyler to the west. Not only do the businessmen bring their wares, but they also bring their salesmen. From the salesmen come stories worn with use in the cities.

Thus, the custom of telling stories at Canton's First Monday is a tradition within a tradition, and one that serves both communal and personal needs.

I started collecting tales in Canton in the Fall of 1972 while studying with J. Mason Brewer, a man who taught me much about the folktale. I found out early that people in Canton do not like tape recorders, so I wrote down the stories I heard as soon as I could after they were told. I lost some stories that way. Trading folk like to drink when they tell stories. Some nights I was lucky to get home. The first story I heard was told in the back of a pickup truck on a cool, rainy November night. Some crazy country cousins, between cases of beer, talked to me about ancient relatives from the Canton area.

First Monday tales come in a variety of types and motifs. A collector can choose from stories of "deception" and "animals," to stories of "exaggeration" and the "wonderful hunt." However, to write of the "types" and "motifs" of the Canton stories makes me a little uneasy. Above everything else they are honest stories in an old tradition, a tradition that is at once as ancient as forefathers and as close as family. I think of the tellers as brothers and sisters and not sources. If the tellers are not poets, they must be poems.

STUBBORN MULE
Told by Truman Fincher

I remember once when my father and I went in to Tradin' Day. We lived out west of town on a farm and Papa wanted to trade an old horse that wasn't worth nothin' for a mule. He needed a mule for plowin' or something. Well, we took our old horse in on Sunday afternoon—

walked him up to town. Back in those days the horses were sold up around the square; you didn't have to go way down on the highway.

Papa found several guys that had mules for sale but none of them wanted to trade for an old horse like ours was. But those people usually come to make a deal so he finally found a man to trade with for a mule. Only the mule was sorta like our horse—he didn't look like he was much account for nothin'.

Well, we started back home with our old mule and we found along the way that he lived up to the way he looked. Just after we left town the thing stopped right in the middle of the road—it was just dirt but still it was the road. Papa was awful upset and first wanted to take it back to town. But the mule wouldn't even budge, much less turn around and head back to town. So Papa began to think about what he could do.

There was a corn field full of big roastin' ears next to the road. When Papa saw them he started across the road and left me with that dumb old mule.

I asked him where he was going. But he didn't answer me and headed over to a big stalk and pulled off a long ear of corn. He began to peel off the shuck and came back over to me next to the mule.

"I always heard it would work," he said.

I thought he was goin' to feed it to the critter and this would make him go on home. But when he finished shucking the corn he stuck it in the mule's ear. That old mule looked over at us as if he didn't know what was goin' on. He blinked a couple of times; Papa hit him on the rump and said git. We didn't have to stop another time all the way home.

After that whenever that mule took a notion he didn't want to work, we put corn in his ear and he went on.

THE SPOTLESS MULE
Told by C. C. Reed

Once there was the guy who came to First Monday with a mule to sell. This mule wasn't worth much and this guy wanted to get rid of him real bad. So he tried everything he could to get rid of Jess—that was the mule's name—he tried everything he knew to trade him off. Nobody wanted him though.

This man wanted to get rid of Jess so bad he decided he would come early next time and see what the other traders were doing to get rid of their mules. So he come real early next month and walked around and listened to the other traders makin' deals. He didn't like what he heard. The other traders were saying the same thing he had said last month: how good the animals were. They were the best mules in the county, they said.

So this guy that wanted to get rid of his mule Jess decided he would have to think of something new and original to tell the customers. This wasn't an easy job for this guy, 'cause he was just a farmer, growed up and lived here all his life. But he sat down and started thinking. He thought real hard for a long time.

There were some kids came along about that time—kids that went over at Canton High School. One of these kids was talking about this pretty girl, the prettiest girl in the school. A lot of the kids must not have washed their faces back then because this one kid was talking about this pretty girl and said she looked good because she had such clean and clear skin on her face.

This set the guy with the mule Jess to thinking.

About that time a man came up and started looking at the mule. Jess was eating some grass on the east side of the courthouse.

"This here is a real good mule," Jess's owner said to the man. "He ain't got a pimple on him."

SQUIRREL PUP
Told by C. C. Reed

My wife and I went down to the Dog Grounds one Sunday afternoon. It was First Monday. We didn't really know what we wanted but we had been talking about buying me a hunting dog for a long time. So we just got in our pickup and went on down to see what they had.

Most of the dog men do their tradin' on Saturday and then they have a dance on Saturday night to celebrate their deals. A lot of them go home Sunday morning because a lot of them have to drive so far. We got dog men that come from all over America to buy and sell and trade dogs in Canton. I've seen license plates from Georgia and Utah down at the Dog Grounds. But even though they do most of the tradin' on Saturday, there are still a lot of dogs around on Sunday for sale. I have to work on Saturdays so I couldn't go down then.

Well, me and the wife park our pickup truck as near to the Grounds as we can and then walk down to look over the dogs. There were some real fine huntin' dogs down there this Sunday. We saw a bunch that we would like to have had.

We came upon this one guy who had his pickup parked down on the Grounds. He must have been there since early Friday to have such a good parkin' place. This guy had a toothbrush in his mouth like a lot of the dog dealers do. He was really working that toothbrush. I think it was hackberry. When we came up to him all his dog pens were empty. He didn't have any dogs except this one puppy up in the cab of his truck.

"What you got that dog up in the cab for?" I asked him.

He kinda looked at me as if I was some fool or something and went on chewin' and workin' that toothbrush. Then he stopped.

"I don't want that dog to catch cold," he said.

"What's he some kinda special dog or something?" I asked.

He looked at me again as if I didn't have much brains and worked with his toothbrush.

"That pup is about the most special squirrel dog you'll ever lay your eyes on," he said.

The wife and I went over and took a closer look. That was a pretty good looking pup. He was about a year old the owner said and already he could tree a squirrel better than any dog he had ever seen. Other dogs would wander off after they treed a squirrel, but this pup would stay under that tree 'till hell froze over, he said. My wife thought he looked good too but she didn't know nothin' about squirrels.

This owner went on and on about the pup: how the pup was out sniffin' for squirrel a week after he was born; how the pup had huntin' in his blood; how you could see the huntin' instinct in him; and how he would never sell such a dog.

I bought him right there on the spot. Paid a good bit for a squirrel dog. We took him out of the pickup and I wrapped him in my coat so he wouldn't get a cold. It was January and pretty cold. I didn't put him back in the back on the way home but let him set up in the front with us.

We took real good care of him when we got him home and forever 'til he died of old age.

But that dog would never leave our yard except to come in the house.

And he never treed a squirrel in his whole life.

THE EASY-GOIN' MULE

Once there was this feller who bought himself a mule over at Canton square. He wasn't very smart, hadn't been out in the country very long and didn't know too much about farm animals. He'd moved over from Oklahoma City, bein' born and raised there until his old aunt died and left him some land just outside Canton.

This feller came on into town one Monday and bought the first mule he came across. The man that sold the mule to him wasn't no slick talker or anything like that; he just left outside some important details about that mule when he sold him.

When the new man in town got home with his mule he showed him to his family and he just sat out and watched his new mule awhile. First the mule just stood when he was put in the pen next to the barn. That mule didn't do nothin' for about an hour, just stood there. But the next thing you know this mule started walking around and running into the fence and the barn. He'd wheel around and the first thing you knowed, he's up against something else.

Well, the new man he couldn't figger out what was goin' on so he went back up into town and found the man who'd sold him the mule.

"That mule you sold me," he said, "that mule keeps running into things."

"That so?" the former owner said.

"Uh-huh. He ran into the fence and butted his head against the barn."

"That so?" the former owner said.

"That mule you sold me couldn't be blind could it?" the new man asked.

The former owner spit a running dribble of tobacco out of his mouth, looked real serious at the new man, and said,

"That mule ain't blind. He just don't give a damn."

ANTIQUE DIRT-DOBBER NESTS

We had an old boy from Oklahoma come down one month. He was dirt poor and you could see it in his clothes. Didn't have hardly anything but rags on his back and his old boots looked more like sandals they had so many holes in them. Have you ever seen any high-topped sandals?

Come to find out he'd heard about First Monday and about all these people comin' down here and making lots of money selling just about anything and everything. So he came down here going to look things over and find out what he could see. He came down in an old wagon and left his wife and kids at home. It was a business trip you see. He came down on Saturday and slept Saturday night down with the dog-traders. One of the dog owners told us later the Oklahoma man had said he had fourteen kids. I wouldn't doubt. He looked some poor.

Come Sunday afternoon this old boy was wandering around the grounds looking things over trying to figure out what he had at home he could bring back and sell himself. We have some pretty sharp sellers and traders come to First Monday, and one of them spotted this Oklahoman a mile off. He was a man selling tools—screw drivers, and hammers and things. He saw this guy coming up and pulled a dirt-dobber nest off from the underneath side of his truck bed. He sat that nest up right in the middle of his tools.

"What's this?" asked the Oklahoman.

"This is an antique dirt-dobber nest," the man with the tools replied.

"How much do you want for it?"

"I usually sell them for five dollars, but you can have this one for two-fifty."

"Hell, I don't want to buy one. I just wanted to see how much they sell for. I'm a rich man. I got a whole barn full of those things up home."

B. L. Barrett with Y rod.

Buddy McCool with L rods.

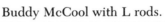

FOLLOWING THE FORKED STICK

Photographs and Text
by Archie P. McDonald

"And the Lord spake unto Moses . . . Take the rod, and gather thou the assembly together . . . and speak ye unto the rock before their eyes . . . and thou shalt bring forth to them water out of the rock: . . . And Moses took the rod from before the Lord . . . And Moses lifted up his hand, and with his rod he smote the rock twice: and water came out abundantly." (Numbers 20:7-11)

A few modern dowsers suggest that the above quotation qualifies Moses as the first recorded water-witch. This quotation may be advanced to lend Biblical authority to their own practices, or it may be the assertion of claim to an act of succession akin to the "laying on of hands" of the Apostolic Succession, depending on your viewpoint. And that is one thing you are bound to have when dowseing is introduced, for there are few, if any, open minds on the subject. There are, to be sure, varying degrees of belief and agnosticism, ranging from the evangelical to those who cry fraud and nonsense.

Despite the Moses theory, it is more likely that dowseing is of much later origin. Extensive anthropological research has found no evidence of its practice among the primitive (or cultured) peoples of Africa, the Orient, Polynesia, or North or South American Indians prior to the arrival of Europeans. It is almost certainly a Western cultural phenomenon, and probably is restricted to the last five hundred years. Since this corresponds to the discovery of practically everything since the wheel, it cannot be simply dismissed that the forces which produce the reaction were not present before then; it is possible that they were present but not applied. While it is true that the Roman term, *virgula divina*, is the origin of the words "divining rod," the Romans apparently used the wood for auguring, rather than for water or mineral location, and even though the Greek word *rhabdos*, or rod, and *manteia*, or divination, are root words for rhabdomancy, a modern term for dowseing, there is no particular evidence that the Greeks put either the words or the practice to common use. The earliest historical reference to dowseing comes from monastic records, some dating to the fifteenth century. At first the practice seemed to be accepted as a Godly gift with little criticism, but there were always some who suspected the hand of the devil, and an ecclesiastical and academic controversy as to the supernatural aspect of dowseing, now four centuries old, was begun. Among the first claims for the influence of God were those by early German miners who believed that the rod could help them find deposits of ore only if the rod had been cut on St. John's Day and was properly baptisted.

Many still question the "divine" aspects of the rod's use and attribute its power to the devil, one of the folk-explanations of the term "Witch," but this has never stopped the practice. By the beginning of the eighteenth century it was employed in every European country and through their expanding influence was exported to the frontiers of their empires. It is not known when dowseing was first introduced into the British colonies in America, but it was likely as early as the seventeenth century. References in colonial newspapers and religious tracts tend to equate locating water by means of the rod with witchcraft, hence water-witching, but others claim that the words were derived from the colonists' preference for witch-hazel twigs to use in the process. In any event, the dichotomy of the terms "divine" and "witch" are part of the folk reaction to the practice. Whatever the true source, water-witching is presently the most commonly used reference, followed by dowseing (preferred in Europe), divining, smelling, channel surveying, wishing for water, prophesying, doodle-bugging (usually in reference to oil or minerals), or radiesthesia, a French derivative used in medical divining.

Dowsers are presently divided between two similar but differently purposed groups. There are, for instance, the rural dowsers who generally limit their search to water. The stimulus is usually their own or a neighbor's need for water to sustain their agricultural efforts. There is no way to know accurately just how many rural dowsers there are now, but a survey conducted in 1957 estimated that there were then more than eighteen thousand. It is reasonable to assume that their numbers have increased. This survey, conducted by sociologists Ray Hyman and Elizabeth G. Cohen and others on a grant from

Harvard University, found that the distribution of rural dowsers was in direct proportion to the aridity of a region or was affected by other factors which made the obtaining of sufficient water supplies difficult. Need, in other words, produced method, especially whenever modern geologic techniques were uncertain or had previously failed.

A second category is urban dowsers, who seek water, if at all, much less frequently than do their country cousins. They are much more interested in the "why" of dowseing than the "how." They are as apt to be found dowseing for the fun of it as for something practical, to be engaged in experiments to further the pure knowledge of the practice, to be seen in the search for gold, using new techniques, experimenting with Kirlian photography, or dowseing from maps and even photographs. And above all, they are organized. The rural dowser works generally alone, and if appreciated at all, it is by the few for whom he has found precious water where it was scarce. The urbanite seeks his own kind, though he is often quick to charge perfidy if he suspects it, and there frequently is an ego clash when rods do not respond alike. It is difficult to say what bonds the dowsers together. For some it is perhaps the herd instinct, for others the desire to be with those who share their interest and to further their own skill by learning from their colleagues, and for a few it might be just to get their backs together to face a hostile and doubting world.

Whatever their motive, organizations for dowsers abound. Virtually every country in Europe supports at least one society, and most publish journals. Among the best and most active is the British Society of Dowsers which ties together a membership from throughout the Commonwealth. Closer to home is the American Society of Dowsers, headquartered in Danville, Vermont. This group began its operation in 1960 and is a "non-profit, non-commercial, non-stock, educational organization international in scope and membership." Its membership is open to all, it claims no corporate view of dowseing, and it has adopted no standard technique. Its purpose is to gain for dowseing "a stature of dignity and authority," to win for it prestige and respect, to help members with dowseing problems, to give assistance to beginners, and to disseminate dowseing knowledge and information in order that the process may become more accepted and used. A common belief among dowsers is that the power, whatever its source, is not evil and should be used for the good of as many people as possible. The society holds an annual meeting in September and regularly attracts the faithful as well as sceptics who find amusement in an acre full of dowsers walking hither and yon, rods of various kinds leading them about and indicating to each evidently whatever he asks of it. At present the executive of the Society is Norman Leighton, who has gone to great lengths to invite sceptics to come and become believers.

Dowseing powers are found in both sexes and all ages, and the tools of the trade are varied. The familiar Y-shaped or forked stick is probably the most prevalently used implement because of tradition and availability. If colonials believed in the witchhazel and monks insisted on baptism, such exclusiveness has been abandoned in favor of utility. Modern dowsers can use peach, willow, elm, apple, dogwood, beech, maple, pinon or juniper (where the others are scarce), elderberry, and probably anything else including redwood if they could reach the limbs. This is because most modern dowsers do not believe that the tool is what attracts the substance being sought. Most regard it only as a tool, like a needle on a gauge, while they are themselves the receiving agent. Many have progressed beyond wood, even if they prefer the Y. Forked implements of whale bone, plastic, nylon, or even metal can be made, purchased from a dowseing society, or rarely, from a commercial store. They range in size from a few inches, which is easily transportable, to several feet. Other dowsers prefer what are called angle rods, an L shaped tool made of metal and used in pairs. Still others like a pendulum, frequently made of a cup to hold samples of the item being sought and then suspended to await the signal that the search has been successful. Some like a straight stick, and one New Yorker used a kitchen broom. The choice is purely one of preference, not performance, for all have claimants who hold that they will locate water, oil, gold, missing persons, distinguish between different substances, and perform other feats.

Techniques naturally vary, even if the end is the same. To use the Y shaped stick, the dowser grasps the doubled end of the stick with his thumb planted against the ends, which should be angled for comfort. His palms should be up, his elbows held firmly to the body. The rod is then tensed upward at approximately a forty-five degree angle from his body. He may then begin to slowly walk over the area, but above all he must concentrate on what is being sought. When he does so adequately the stick will dip in the direction of, let us say, a vein of water. The dip will begin when he enters the magnetic field of the vein and will point straight down when he is over it. By approaching it from several directions he can ascertain breadth and depth of the vein. A more practiced dowser such as Henry Gross can obtain the same information from the rod by simply asking for it. Obviously it does not speak to him; rather, it continues to dip as he asks "Is it ten feet? Is it fifteen feet?," and so forth, until he exceeds the depth that the rod has discerned. He then backs up until the proper depth is reached.

The L rods are grasped loosely in pistol fashion, with the thumbs pressed together. Again, the dowser moves forward, concentrating on what he is seeking until the rods cross in front of him. This method is often used to locate underground lines for utility companies when their maps are inaccurate or absent.

The pendulum behaves quite differently. Water (or oil) is placed in the cup and the cup is suspended with lines that are held at a distance of about one foot, grasped between thumb and forefinger. Whenever the pendulum is over the vein it will begin to rotate, usually clockwise.

As impressive as these feats may be, they are regarded as rather elementary by the more experienced dowsers. These selected few claim to be able to find veins and even domes of water at great distances from maps, and a very few claim that they can dowse character or personality from photographs. It is these latter claims that separate the "natural" dowsers from those who verge on supernatural themes. All that most dowsers claim for their art is that it is an empiric method for finding something, usually water, and all they ask is an honest and fair opportunity to make it work. "Let me cut a stick," they will say, "and I will show you where to dig a well. If you do what I say you will find the water just where I say it is." Explanations for lack of success include the failure to follow instructions or perhaps damage to the vein in the digging, especially if it is done with heavy equipment which crushes the earth and seals the vein, at least temporarily.

Assuming that it is at least an empiric method, why does it work? Most geologists claim that it really does not. They suggest that dowsers are really amateur hydrologic engineers whose sticks always tell them to dig where the best signs are anyway. Others believe that the entire earth is underlain by water where the rains of past years have percolated to "table" level and can be found by a drill bit nearly anywhere with a great deal more certainty than an above ground stick that is thirsty. Dowsers refer to such holdings as seepage water and find it insufficient in quantity and quality. The few physicists who have conducted experiments in this area adhere to the magnetic theory. All atomic substances, they say, are surrounded by a magnetic field. When a "receiver" locates a "sender," contact is made and the rod dips. It dips because the "receiver," when activated, conveys impulses through the dowser's nervous system which cause an involuntary muscular response. But the dowser snorts, "Look at my hands. I hold the rod firmly and it turns in my hands but my hands do not move; even if I try to hold the rod, it turns anyway." And so the argument goes on.

If dowseing is an empiric method, it should be at least observed on its own ground. Dowsers are not as hard to find as might be imagined. Even in crowds of sophisticates you can usually find one that will admit half proudly that he can do it, even as he casts sheepish glances to see who might be listening. Some think they can do it because they have inherited the talent, such as father to son, female to male and back to female in as many generations, or even the seventh son of a seventh son. All have at least observed others before becoming interested enough to see if they could do it themselves. Two dowsers who proved most cooperative where Harmon T. ("Buddy") McCool, of Nacogdoches, and B. L. Barrett of Beaumont and Newton County, Texas. McCool says that he can find any underground water that is moving. He first learned that he had the talent when his grandfather encouraged him to try the rod and offered helpful advice. Later he also observed a witcher employed by an oil company for which he worked in south Texas. When asked why it works, he said, "It is just something that happens," but he believes that in his case it is because he has the ability to concentrate hard enough on the vein or line being sought. He subscribes to the magnet field theory, but rejects the involuntary-muscular-response concept because he has tried to use his wrist muscles to stop the L rods he prefers and cannot. He is a maintenance supervisor for a large state institution, and has found several buried lines which did not show on the utility maps, saving his employer both money and time.

A more extensive use of the dowseing art has been accomplished by Barrett, whom I have observed on numerous occasions. Barrett works rapidly but his movements are smooth and athletic. His countenance is a study in concentration as he constantly tensions his rod into the search position until he senses a response to the questions he has been silently putting to it; then he will suddenly veer in the direction of the pull. He will occasionally break the silence to articulate the information he has been registering; then he is off again, following his forked stick.

Barrett first learned the techniques of witching from a brother-in-law. He had heard of the finding of water by the method while growing up in the saw-mill towns of East Texas, but he was in his early fifties when necessity drove him to give it a try. He became involved in a recreational subdivision along the Sabine River's Toledo Bend Lake, and he promised water to the purchasers of his land. He consulted several professional well drilling companies, including Lane Wells, but could receive no guarantee of water in sufficient quantity north of the Newton County line, where his property was located. When his brother-in-law's early efforts proved insufficient, he took over the task himself and found that the rod worked well for him. He stuck to the high ground on the belief that the water would be closer to the surface there because erosion had carried some soil into the valleys. Even if he found water at the lower elevations, he figured, the drilling costs would be higher. On a formation known locally as Hickory Ridge his rod told him that there was water at twenty-one feet and that it would yield sixteen gallons per minute. Later he discovered another source that would yield forty-two gallons per minute at a depth of forty-five feet. The drilling bit proved him right on both counts. Barrett believes that the rod worked accurately for him because he had a strong desire and a need to produce the water. He also is of the opinion that the ability to find water is aided by the benefit that will be achieved for mankind, not an uncommon thought among dowsers. He later found water in an area known as Scrapping Valley on a site where no water had previously been discovered despite the efforts of others stretching over one hundred years. But Barrett's most interesting use of the rod, again born of necessity, came in his discovery of water in a high, mountainous, arid region of southwestern Colorado.

Several years ago he acquired a 300 acre tract surrounded by the San Juan National Forest. He intended to subdivide it, and provide a forty acre lake. He also promised to secure a source of potable water for his purchasers. Barrett had no previous experience here as he had in East Texas, but he was confident that the water would be there. He obtained a permit to drill from the appropriate state agency, and returned to Texas to his regular job at a chemical plant. His son hired a driller and together they punched three holes in the soil and rock. Each yielded water, but in insufficient amounts. By telephone he learned that the area did not appear to have the necessary water. He spread his large map of the area on the floor and made a pendulum. After considerable concentration and study of the map, he telephoned his son to move to a lower site. Water, he said, would be there and in sufficient quantities. He predicted depth and gallonage from his map divining, and when the bit hit the anticipated depth, there was water. The driller continued to bore and nearly lost the bit. When the well was brought in at forty feet, it yielded forty gallons per minute without dropping the level.

Why is he able to locate water? Barrett believes that the water, along with other substances, sends out magnetic waves and that when he tunes to them properly through concentration, he receives them much in the same fashion as does a radio. Unlike the impulse-brain-nerve-muscle concept of the physicists, he believes it is wave-rod-muscle-nerve-brain, and it is at this final point that he determines what he has found. He tries to stop the rod when it is working so as not to give in to impulse, but cannot. He also believes that he improves with experience. Barrett thinks that dowseing is a very natural, rather than super-natural, gift-talent, which is his as other men are painters and sculptors. He also believes that a clean mind and a noble purpose are helpful, and that greed would cause increased failure.

After reading both sides of the argument, talking with dowsers and scientists, and above all, holding the stick and watching it turn, one is compelled to make some out-on-a-limb statements. First, as an empiric method, dowseing seems to be effective more often than it is not if all directions of the dowsers are followed. Second, most dowsers are convinced people, doubting not in the least their ability despite the snickers and jeers that often greet their work. Finally, just because I cannot understand it or explain it, I am not prepared to say categorically that it does not have some adequate, plausible, believable, scientific explanation which may some day be discovered. After all, I have never really comprehended music and voices and images wafting their way through the air and finding a home in a box in my den.

BIBLIOGRAPHY

Barrett, L. K. and E. Z. Vogt. "Urban American Dowsers," *Journal of American Folklore*, LXXXII (July, 1969), 195–213.

Cone, E. F. "The Divining Rod Made Respectable," *Scientific American*, CXXV (September 24, 1929), 219.

Hoffman, E. B. (translator), written by von Klenckowstroem. "Problem of the Divining Rod," *Scientific American*, CXXXXIX (November, 1933), 218–219.

Hyman, R. and E. G. Cohen. "Water-witching in the United States," *American Sociological Review*, XXII (December, 1957), 719–724.

Ingalls, A. G. "Along Came Physics," *Scientific American*, CLXIV (February, 1941), 68.

Reddick, T. M. "Dowsing Is Nonsense," *Harpers Magazine*, CCXXX (July, 1951), 62–68.

Stephenson, H. K. "Witching Wand and Doodlebugs," *Atlantic Monthly*, CLXXXII (September, 1948), 86–87.

Vogt, E. Z. "Interviewing Water-dowsers," *American Journal of Sociology*, LXII (September, 1956), 198.

———. "Water Witching: An Interpretation of a Ritual Pattern in a Rural American Community," *Scientific Monthly*, LXXV (September, 1952), 175–186.

——— and P. Golde, "Some Aspects of the Folklore of Water Witching in the United States," *Journal of American Folklore*, LXXI (October, 1958), 519–531.

FAITH HEALING

from *Loblolly*
by Freda Hardin, Norbert Korzeniewski,
Tommy Hooper, and David Hammers

W ITH a name like Lincoln King a man's got to be either black or Yankee, and Linc's the latter. He's an Up-East school teacher who came to the little East Texas town of Gary and showed a bunch of Southern kids how to learn more about their land and their people and their traditions than most of their elders knew. Linc's wife started it all when she discovered a copy of *Foxfire*, the very successful folklife publication put out by Eliot Wiggington's Rabun Gap, Georgia, students. She showed the book to Linc, who soon established the Foxfire concept as a teaching method in his high school history class. Since then the Gary High School class of '76 has done more in the collection of oral history and folklore than most college classes that I know about. They've visited, watched, and listened to half the mature population of Panola and Shelby Counties and have had more luck getting people to talk into tape recorders than most professionals. Their youth must be in their favor. And their interest. That's the main thing; they are truly interested in the people and their stories and they show it. Their transcriptions, when they get around to publishing the interviews, aren't always consistent in spelling and punctuation, but they are understandable, and their stories catch the flavor of a lot of rich living in the piney woods.

When the time comes that future generations want to know about the customs and traditions and ways of life in East Texas generally, they can find what they are looking for in the collections of *Loblolly*. And if you are interested in seeing what a group of high school folklorists and social historians are doing today, send $5.00 for a year's subscription to *Loblolly*, Box 88, Gary, Texas 75643. —Editor.

We've never had an article on faith healing before even though we've talked to others about it. We got the idea originally from our friend, Rev. DuBose of the Eastside Missionary Baptist Church in Gary. He told us that his mother was a faith healer, so we decided to interview her to find out more about the subject. Her name is Linnie DuBose. She is seventy-seven and now lives in Pineland, Texas. She has had a busy life of service for others, including a skill as a midwife.

Some treat the talents and beliefs regarding faith healers with a large grain of salt. That is up to the individual. But we have talked to several who had warts removed by healers, and they certainly believe. Linnie DuBose has a deep and abiding faith in the Lord. She gives all credit to Him for whatever she has been able to do to help others. This aid has been freely given for she knows that not all possess her gifts.

She told of her ability to draw fire out of a person, the idea being that after a person has been burned the fire continues to flame within. Unless it is drawn out it makes recovery slower and more painful. Thrash (or thrush) is a childhood disease with symptoms of blisters around and inside the mouth. This can spread to the mother if the baby is breast fed, and if not cured the child could eventually die.

We have never seen any of the healers we've met actually at work. But they all radiate such a sincerity of faith in their gift and in the Divine power behind it all that one can lose much of the skepticism he might have had.

LOBLOLLY—We understand you can heal by faith and wonder how you got that power?
Mrs. DuBose—I got it from the Lord.
LOBLOLLY—Are Bible verses used?
Mrs. DuBose—For stopping bleeding it is, but I can't remember where. I think it's the sixteenth chapter of Ezekiel.
LOBLOLLY—Do you remember where you got the ability to do that? Did someone tell you or did you just find out?
Mrs. DuBose—Found out through the Lord. I found others done it too. I don't think I ask for unreasonable things of the Lord. I don't think that's right. I broke my arm, broke my ribs, sprained my foot, and I have a crooked spine to go with it. Straining through a lifetime of working has done it and I put that all on myself. The Lord did not do

it. He can only help me deal with it. He put these herbs and medi-
cines here and give us knowledge and understanding how to use them
you know. Well he didn't give everyone the same power. Some know
more than others.

LOBLOLLY—How would you stop bleeding?

Mrs. DuBose—By the verse of the Bible. You don't have to touch
them. You just talk to the Lord and it's all right. It stops the bleeding
quick, I understand. But I never did this myself.

LOBLOLLY—What about thrash?

Mrs. DuBose—Why, you could have an old piece of bacon, and use it
to make Christ's cross on the bottom of an old smutty skillet. It could
be any kind of meat you could get good and smutty from the skillet.
Then use it to rub the baby's mouth real good and then give the
meat to a black dog and forget about it. It's cured, just like that. Of
course it takes time to heal up, but then it will not break out again.
It's got to have time to heal. His mouth gets smutty and his lips because it's supposed to, but you don't go wash it off. You let it wear off.

Another thing is if you hold a baby up in the sunlight and get it's
mouth open. Let the sun shine down it's little mouth before he's three
days old and he won't never have thrash.

Another thing you can do if you had a little baby with thrash and it
caused your breast to be infected or something like that, it could be
rubbed and it will go down. It will do that; I seen it tried. Another
way you can cure that and I think it will cure the thrash too is that
some takes a baby down into the woods and get some kind of leaf and
rub it's mouth. I don't know the details about that.

A man or a woman can take and smother three of these things they
call mold. The mold runs under the ground, you know, and makes
them little runners. You can take and smother three of them and you
can blow it in the baby's mouth and cure the thrash. Or you can rub
the mother's breast and it will go down if it is risen.

LOBLOLLY—Have you treated anybody for snake bite?

Mrs. DuBose—Well I haven't treated a snake bite but I have treated
for wasps and things like that.

LOBLOLLY—How would you do that?

Mrs. DuBose—Well I was told how by somebody. I forgot who but
it will work on the wasp bites. I shouldn't tell for fear of losing the
power. But I don't ever use it anymore. But if it's the Lord's will I guess
I could. You rub your hand on the bite and say:

'Julia, Julia, are you dead?
Go way down south and come no more
And this we ask in the name of the Father, and of the Son and of the
    Holy Ghost.
Amen and amen.'
Just like that! But you got to have the faith there.
LOBLOLLY—Do you have a cure for bruises?
Mrs. DuBose—Naw, not exactly, but if you got bruised and it swells
up real bad, just go out and pick you some buds off some tender sas-
safras bud. And beat 'em up and put you some ice water on 'em, make
you a poltice out of 'em. Put it on the bruises; it'll draw every bit of
that swellin' out. Best you can do for swellin'.
LOBLOLLY—Did you use sassafras tea too?
Mrs. DuBose—That's right; it's good blood medicine. It keeps your
blood thinned up to where you can stand the heat during the summer.
It tastes good too. I've got some cured roots there in the kitchen.
You can buy 'em in the store now. You can tell a sassafras tree by the
smell.
LOBLOLLY—Do you know about getting rid of warts too?
Mrs. DuBose—Yea, it's done kinda like a snake bite. You have one on
your hand and you just say:
  'Wart, wart, go away,
  Go away down south and come no more.'
You forget about it and next thing you know you look there and it's
gone.
LOBLOLLY—How do you draw fire?
Mrs. DuBose—Blow on it and talk to it. Like you was burnt on your
hand anywhere. Don't make no difference where, you can blow on it.
Just do it as hard as you can and talk just as many words as you can as
long as that breath lasts. Get another long breath and blow again till
you get it all recited. And do that till it quits burning. It'll quit.
Say:
  'Come out fire, come in frost,
  Follow thy Lord, thy Son, and thy Holy Ghost.
  Amen.'
You may have to get breath between words and syllables like that
but blow just as hard as you can with your breath on that place. And
it'll work, does for me. The directions to that is not to tell nobody who
is related to you. You can cure your kin just as long as you don't tell

'em. I learned to do this from an old lady named Fanny Bell Wright. She's dead now.

One of the neighbor children got burnt pretty bad and they sent for me and my maw. She could take the fire out too and we both worked on that child half a day. We cured it too.

When I lived at Buna there was a child who had walked through a bed of hot coals barefooted. He had hopped through on one foot. He just burnt it real bad and hadn't wore a shoe for a week. His mother heard about me, that I could do that, and she brought that little boy to me. I worked on him an hour or two that night. And she went on back home and she said next day he put on a shoe and never had more trouble with it.

LOBLOLLY—Do you have any other cures?

Mrs. DuBose—I know another thing that might be of help to anybody and anybody can fix it. And that is with this poltice outfit when you're hurtin' and can't get no relief or nothin'. One time a man got a hook caught in his side while workin' in the woods. It tore the stripin' loose between his ribs and his intestines and air got in there. Well, the doctor doctored him two weeks and he couldn't hardly bear to be turned over and he couldn't turn himself. He thought at first he had pneumonia but he didn't. They wanted to send him to Lufkin. But before that happened, a doctor's wife who was livin' close to me wanted to fix a poltice and put on him. So she took a box of dry mustard, two boxes of flour, a half cup of syrup, and a half cup of vinegar. She stirred that all up together and got it hot. She put it on him and it eased him. That will remove pain of pneumonia and stuff when everything else fails. Keep it warm. You may have to take it off every once in awhile. If not, it'll blister. And wash him, put some oil on him, warm the poltice and put it back. Get him easy—but it'll work.

LOBLOLLY—Can you tell us about the chicken pox?

Mrs. DuBose—Well, you just make sure you got your chickens penned up. Next mornin' take whoever is sick out there and let the chickens fly over 'em. They say it will work, cure 'em. I never did try that.

But I've tried this other. Kill an old black hen and scald her. Pick her like you was gonna eat her. But anyway, you save that water. Usually it's children that has the pox. But anyway you save that water and give 'em a bath in it. Give the kid a bath and it will cure the chicken pox.

Oh yes, I've also used a cure for the itch. My kids all had it. I just got some sulfur and grease and rubbed it on 'em. Some tell to have 'em wear their clothes for nine days, then burn the clothes. They think it will cure the itch. I done my kids that way and it didn't work. Someone told me if I'd put the kids in runnin' water the first three mornings in May before sunup it would cure it. That's what I done and they got all right. Just like I tell you, you've got to have faith in anything before it'll work.

Boil hives are what kids have when they are little. Well when everything else fails, give 'em all kinds of tea. Make it out of all kinds of stuff nearly for the hives. When all that fails, take a razor blade and between the baby's shoulder blades make Christ's cross—just enough for it to bleed a little, not deep. Give that child that blood. Get it up with a spoon or something' another and give it to that child. And that'll cure the boil hives. We call it scarifyin' 'em.

We also went to visit with our old friend Ollie Prince. She had earlier helped us in making hominy. We had heard from her grandson that she had the power to stop bleeding both with people and with animals. She is also of a strong faith and her children from personal experience are thankful of her gift.

Ollie Prince—Oh yea, there's a verse in the Bible that you can repeat it over three times. I can show it to you boys but not girls or I'd lose my power to heal. My boys had been cut a many time and I stopped it. One time J. W. was about ten or eleven years old; he cut his toe off; cut it completely off and it was just a bleeding. He was runnin' up to the house. His sister was just a hollerin', "Mother, get the Bible, Mother, get the Bible." And I got the Bible, read that verse over and it stopped. One time down here at the Trades Day, Mr. Youngblood had a horse down there that was just a bleedin' and J. W. come and got me and said, "Mother, go down to that horse and stop it from bleedin'." I did and the bleeding stopped. It's done by faith and that verse from the Bible.

We made a new friend when we called on Sybil Whiddon. She is also a neighbor and proved to be most cooperative in answering our questions. She was reticent in getting too specific about her gift of healing but shared some of her experiences with us. And she repeated what others had already told us, that the power to heal depends on a strong faith in the Lord.

Sybil Whiddon—This old man, Mr. Eaton, he had been our friend for a long time and everybody that would get burned would go to him to get the fire talked out. When my oldest child was about three or four years old he was climbing up on the mantle and fell in the fire place, in the bed of ashes, you know, the coals. And I took him to the man. Well, he cured him. Now if nobody believes in it there's nothing to it. But if anybody believes in prayer they ought to believe in this. People laughed at me sometimes but I won't tell anybody about it unless I trust the person real good. 'Cause if they don't believe in it and they don't seem worthy of my trust I won't tell them. This old man, he told me of his gift 'cause he trusted me and didn't think he would live much longer. He said he wanted to leave the knowledge with me, so he told me. And then if anybody that wants to know how to talk the fire out, well they could come to me and if I thought they were worthy, I would tell them. I could only tell one man, and if I told any more the power would be taken away from me. My mother could stop blood but she told too many people how, so her power passed away from her. It's just a matter of prayer and your belief in God.

One time my little granddaughter got burned on her little hand on the top of a heater. She lived in Deadwood and her mother brought her down to my house when I lived in Joaquin. And she just screamed all the way down there. After I talked the fire out they headed back home, and by the time they got to the river bridge she was asleep.

Another time I just didn't know to put my trust in the incident. Robert Sears married my daughter Brenda. She carried him some coffee one morning when he was in bed and he spilt it on his side. He said, "Go call Mama and talk the fire out." I told Brenda I'd never tried it on the phone but I'd try. And just from her calling me it didn't even blister. And then one of my neighbors, the arm was badly burned, black, and she came over and I talked the fire out. The next morning it wasn't even sore. Just lots of people I've helped.

I don't tell what I say when I'm talking the fire out. I just say it to myself so I won't lose the power. And I blow on the fire while talking.

My mother could stop blood till she told too many people. Anybody, you know, or an animal—she could fix it. She didn't actually have to see them. I have a brother-in-law, he can stop blood. I had a big rising on my leg one time and I was picking at it. It came out spouting; it scared me to death. My husband was in the field so the kids ran to their grandmother's to get my brother-in-law. And it stopped all of a sudden. That's what did it, whatever he said. I can't do that myself but I know others can. My mother found she had lost her power when she tried to help a baby. She couldn't do any good and the doctors couldn't. The baby died. She gave up on it then. She didn't even cure horses any more as she had been able to before.

And this is by God helping and believing in His power. I have been thankful for the gift and being able to help others.

WHITTLER'S BENCH — TENAHA, TEXAS

Photographs and Text by Francis Edward Abernethy

SOMETIMES a man gets the feeling that he's not living life, that it's living him. He cuts the grass, turns around, and there it is whispering to be cut again. He fixes the starter on his car, and the washing machine demands equal time. He spends all his money paying one stack of bills, while another stack stridently insists that it be paid too. He begins to feel that he is running in deep sand, and if he ever slows down all the responsibilities in his life will roll over him and bury him. This is the time, if he has any character, that he will step aside, let it all roll by, and go fishing. Or if that is too much trouble, he can sit down and whittle. Tenaha, Texas, in its infinite wisdom has provided a whittlers' bench for just such an occasion.

Tenaha (of "Tenaha, Timpson, Bobo, and Blair" fame) is in Shelby County, deep in the East Texas pines. It's a small town but it seems satisfied and easy going, and it's what a lot of Houston and Dallas people dream about escaping to. Tenaha is an Indian name and it means "muddy water." One of the whittlers said that the town was called "muddy water" because during the wet years, back when it rained regularly, there was always a pond of red-dirt-muddy water standing between the main street and the railroad tracks. The other whittlers agreed both with the etymology and the fact that it used to rain more.

Tenaha's whittlers' bench is set against the brick east side of Wall Drug Store. It is a weathered-oak two-by-twelve that sits on iron pipe legs. For a long time the bench sat on cedar blocks, but these were slowly whittled away. A part of one of the blocks is still in the wood pile at the end of the bench, still furnishing whittling material for the guests.

132

The whittlers started off by telling me that the bench had been there since The Beginning. Then some fellow in his mid-eighties said that it had been there all his life, or at least as long as he could remember. They finally decided that since somebody was going to write it down that the bench had been there around fifty years. And it has been the popular gathering place for the Tenaha whittling aristocracy for all that time.

Some days, they tell me, the bench is in such demand that a serious whittler can hardly find space to sit down, and he doesn't dare get up once he gets a place. The number of whittlers varied from six to ten the day I visited. Most of the men are retired, between work, or did what they had to do that morning. One of them said that he used to spend his time fishing but he got saved, and had to give up lying, so he took up whittling instead. They are a strong and hardy crew in spite of the large number of years they stack up among themselves. They are proud of the combination of wit, spirit, strength, and age which characterizes them, and they brag enthusiastically on their oldest member, who is ninety-four, still doesn't wear glasses, and drives Tenaha's only taxicab.

They are also proud of their whittling skill. Expert whittling doesn't require a real sharp knife, I learned. In fact, a sharp slicing knife with a long bevel would slice into the wood, which is what a whittler doesn't want to do. A short bevel on a not-too-sharp knife is what is required, one that will plane off long, thin curls of delicate shavings. A real professional can start at one end of his whittling stick and shave a long curl all the way down to the other.

They don't whittle things either, like wooden spoons or fids or candlesticks. Their purpose on that bench is not to create either the useful or the ornamental. They are there asserting their independence and demonstrating their command of their lives by cultivating skill without purpose. They are practicing conspicuous consumption of time, and those of us who speed through Tenaha to make an appointment on time in Shreveport eye them with envy. They know this. They whittle pieces of wood into non-utilitarian forms to show the world that while they are on that bench they don't have to be concerned with clocks or with the frantic struggle to either decorate, maintain, or keep up with life.

Their talk is much like their whittling, an artistic and conspicuous consumption of words. Theirs is one of the few places in our society where conversation is an art form, where telling tales, moralizing, lying, sermonizing, playing with words and figures of speech are practiced and cultivated as an end in themselves. They are masters at the use of colorful and dynamic language, and their speech patterns and dialect will never be diluted or standardized by television, movies, or journalese. And like the whittled stick, their talk is an end in itself and does not require a practical and social application. They can discuss politics, morality, and ethics academically, separated for the time being from the actuality of these things, as a historian might discuss the Napoleonic Wars. Their talk is not an instrument to persuade men to their way of thinking or living or to bring about changes in society. It is talk for the sake of talk, the refinement of man's greatest glory, his gift of speech.

Their daily gathering also satisfies the ancient instinct of males to bond together, to cluster and exalt in their maleness, and to celebrate their masculine command of life and all creatures in it. An interesting female passing by will quicken their conversation considerably and move them out to the edge of the bench, but she is no challenge to their position or territory. The whittlers' bench is a male place, a place of knives and of old hunts and battles and conquests. The uninitiated may sit but he cannot enter.

Ironically, however, the struggle is all. No matter how we might envy the whittlers when we look up from the panic of our own pursuits, most of us would have to be struck down before we could slow down long enough to whittle a decent stick. We are not conditioned for tranquility. Those magic moments are rare when we can truly loaf and invite our souls. They are small glimpses of our fantasies of Paradise, when the lions within us lie down with the lambs. For that reason, because of the rarity of these glimpses, the bench and its occupants stand out as important symbols. Whether they—these men or others like them—are whittling on the city square, at the county courthouse or a filling station, in the park or just in the shade, the whittlers show us that it is possible for a super-charged *homo sapien* in a manicly accelerating machine-of-a-world to step out of the pandemonium for a while, re-assert a little control over his life, and simply savor his humanity.

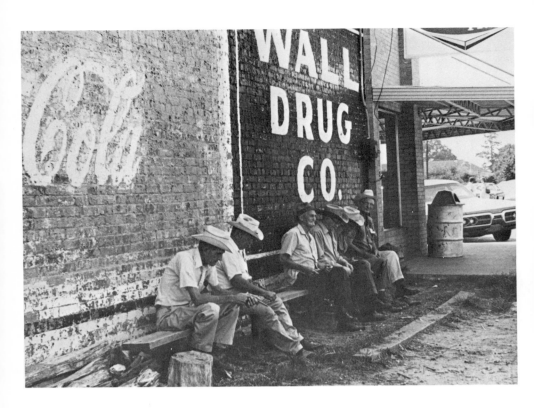

IN MEMORIAM

JOHN Q. ANDERSON
1916–1975

J. FRANK DOBIE dedicated his book on *The Mustangs* to his friend Genardo del Bosque, who often and proudly proclaimed, *"Yo tengo raíces aquí."* Genardo's reference was to the Live Oak County, Texas, ranch where he worked a lifetime. Like Genardo, but in another language and more by intellectual example than simple declaration, John Q. Anderson spent a lifetime demonstrating, "I have roots here." Anderson's Texas was the Panhandle of his birth and the Brazos bottoms and Gulf Coast of his distinguished professorial career.

Born May 30, 1916, in Wheeler, Anderson earned the A.B. degree at Oklahoma State University and served in Europe during World War II, then returned to earn his doctorate and pursued a distinguished career in university teaching and administration. Before his untimely death February 19, 1975, in Houston, he had been awarded the coveted honor of Professor Emeritus at the University of Houston.

During his career he edited and wrote more than a dozen books and monographs; and at the time of his death, he was serving on the editorial board of several journals and as co-editor of *A Bibliography of Southwestern American Literature*. Additionally, he produced more than one hundred articles on American literature and folklore, and made records and tapes of folk songs. Anderson was president (1963–64) of the American Studies Association of Texas, which made him its first "Distinguished Fellow," and held office in many other academic organizations.

Anderson's first love, though, was the Texas Folklore Society in which his wife, Loraine Epps Anderson, shared equal enthusiasm. After serving as president (1955–56) of the Society, he accepted a position on the editorial board that he held until his death. At more than a dozen annual meetings, he presented papers and also participated joyously in the folksinging. Folklorists found his rendition of "Waco Girl" especially appealing.

The distance in Texas from Wheeler in the Panhandle to Houston on the Gulf Coast is even farther intellectually than the hundreds of miles of space. Yet John Q. Anderson traversed the territory admirably without sacrificing either his native or his transplanted roots. Wherever he went, he left his mark.

EDWIN W. GASTON, JR.
Stephen F. Austin State University

J. MASON BREWER
1896–1975

JOHN MASON BREWER of Texas died January 24 in Commerce and was buried in Austin. The nation's leading Negro folklorist lived almost a decade beyond the Biblical three-score and ten; the quality of that life is even more important than the quantity.

The literate world should never repeat the half-truth, "He was a credit to his race." Nor is it sufficient to state, as two Texas historians have done, that Brewer is "the state's only Negro writer of importance." Brewer is a credit to all races—including the black and white—from which his family came.

Six early books of poetry are available in some libraries, and one, *Negrito* (1933), is on sale today. Of his early histories, *Negro Legislators of Texas* (1935) is reprinted. His folk tales are included in five volumes of the TFS now in print, Volumes X to XXXVIII. Not counting minor works, the volumes on which his fame will rest are *Aunt Dicey Tales* (1956), *Dog Ghosts* (1958), *The Word on the Brazos* (1953), *Worser Days and Better Times* (1965), and *American Negro Folklore* (1968), the last still available.

In 1966 I met Mason when I was writing a monograph for the Southwest Writers Series; in 1974 he watched me sign a contract for a biography in the Twayne United States Author Series. Its publication will coincide with the centennial edition of *Who's Who In America*, identifying Brewer for the masses.

For eight years I watched him make history at East Texas State University in folklore scholarship and race relations; he became a major inspiration to me, as he did to innumerable students. That inspiration will remain, through memories, written and unwritten.

It is comforting to think of the many facets of immortality; the influence of a strong personality lives on through those he has taught. J. Mason Brewer is not gone then; he has just "dropped back into the immense design of things."

JAMES W. BYRD
East Texas State University

BERTHA McKEE DOBIE
1890–1974

BERTHA McKEE DOBIE passed away in sleep at the age of 84 on the morning of December 18, 1974. She had consented to go to a hospital for a few days of rest to recover from a minor indisposition. Except for a respiratory disorder and a tendency to tire rather easily, she had been in fairly good health.

The Texas Folklore Society has lost one of its oldest and best friends. Over the years Bertha Dobie assisted the Society in many ways. To the monumental *Legends of Texas* (1924, the second volume edited for the TFS by Frank Dobie), she made three contributions. She wrote articles for later volumes and helped Frank in the burdensome task of editing materials for our Publications. She would do the proofreading when he was involved in a book of his own, and at such times she would take over the correspondence. During the twenty years of Frank's editorship Bertha regularly entertained Society members in her flower-filled yard beside Waller Creek at the close of their Austin meetings.

As late as 1972 she wrote a paper, "On Texas Grasses," for the meeting at College Station.

Bertha was born in Susquehanna County, Pennsylvania, to which her mother had returned to have her first child. After living in various places in Texas, the McKees settled in Velasco, near the mouth of the Brazos. Bertha attended high school in Velasco, perhaps taught for a year, and then entered Southwestern University. Here she met Frank Dobie, whom she married in 1916. Their alma mater has honored them by celebrating more than one "Dobie Day." And the Society will always honor the Dobies. They determined the Society's early character and course while performing various tasks for it and also gave it an esprit de corps by their warmth and encouragement. Their interest in the Society and its affairs continued throughout their lives.

WILSON M. HUDSON
Austin, Texas

JOHN AVERY LOMAX, JR.
1907–1974
MARGARET MARABLE
LOMAX
1908–1973

JOHN AVERY LOMAX, JR., was born in Austin, Texas, June 14, 1907. When John was two years old, his father participated in founding the Texas Folk-Lore Society, and John and the Society grew up together. Although his family moved to Illinois when young John was ten, he had already sunk deep roots into the Texas soil. He loved this state, every hill, valley, river, and town—but most of all, the people.

In 1941, after attending the University of Texas and the Harvard School of Business, John married Margaret Marable, a Clarksville girl who had been born in Hugo, Oklahoma, November 3, 1908. When they met, Mimi was a career girl in New York after matriculating at the

College of Industrial Arts in Denton—now Texas Women's University. After their marriage, John and Mimi decided to settle in Texas and moved to Houston in 1946, where they raised two sons, Joseph Franklin and John Marable. There, also, in 1952 John started the Houston Folklore Society. Never too busy to encourage a young folklorist, John and Mimi were surrogate parents to many.

After a severe stroke broke John's health and shattered his memory, blocking his recall of the hundreds of songs and stories he had acquired through years of devoted collecting, Mimi's courage and care restored him to a greater degree than the doctors believed possible. But her own health failed, and Mimi died on June 24, 1973. A little more than a year later, John followed her on December 12, 1974.

Those of us in the Texas Folklore Society know John and Mimi Lomax as two of the most loyal and committed members the group has ever had. If a job needed doing, they were faithful in the task. And when the singing began, there was John, planted firmly on both feet, his chin pulled back and his big voice reverberating in his barrel chest, his fists clenched and right arm swinging to the rhythm of the tune. Somewhere in the background, Mimi was sitting and smiling, her head nodding and a toe tapping while her fingers busily worked on the ever-present piece of needlepoint, crochet, or knitting. And should John falter, ever so slightly, in beginning the next stanza, Mimi's lips would form the words for him.

We miss them.

JO LYDAY
San Jacinto College

MABEL MAJOR
1894–1974

M ABEL MAJOR was born in Utah, raised and educated in Missouri and came to teach English in Big Spring, Texas, in 1917 because, she said, it was as far away from home as she could get at the time. In 1919 she began a forty-four year teaching career at TCU where she contributed much. After her retirement in 1963 she continued to teach at Baylor and served as a consultant for junior college English departments.

Mabel's contributions were solid and her honors many. Her first piece of writing in Texas appeared in 1923 in *Tone the Bell Easy*. She continued with articles and books the best of which, *Southwest Heritage*, still remains in use as a text book. She was president of the Texas Folklore Society, vice-president of the Texas Institute of Letters, and a Piper Professor.

Mabel's name is linked to that era when folklorists such as Dobie and Boatright began to gather the essence of Texas—its lore. She early staked her claim on a poem, "Lasca" by Frank Desprez, and spent many years even until two weeks before her death on June 3, 1974, in discovering more about it.

As a teacher, Mabel was strict. Not many football players wandered into her classes except by mistake. A student gained a thorough knowledge of Southwest literature, and of Shakespeare and the Victorian writers which were also her specialties. She managed to hang all of them together on the same clothesline and one subject never seemed out of place with the other. Old stove-up cowboys and Rabbi Ben Ezra and Lear had more in common than we at first knew.

Mabel never seemed to get older. She simply grew richer in spirit and experience. She leaned toward scholarly people but never exclusively. She loved the Texas Folklore Society because the group gathered strength from people of widely varied backgrounds and differing opinions.

One of Mabel's favorite lines from "Lasca" expressed the idea that in Texas "one does not drink in little sips"—that life here is great gulps of many things. Her own life was a watering place for many of us. We never went away from her thirsty.

JOYCE ROACH
Keller, Texas

CONTRIBUTORS

FRANCIS EDWARD ABERNETHY is professor of English at Stephen F. Austin State University and is Secretary-Editor of the Texas Folklore Society.

ROBERT MORRIS ABERNETHY is a house carpenter and a student at Stephen F. Austin State University.

JOE ANGLE, recently home from the service, is a law student at Baylor University.

AVA BUSH is a professional home economist and dietitian from Grapeland.

JOHN DANIEL is a talented sculptor and painter and is a professor of art at Stephen F. Austin State University.

JOE S. GRAHAM is a professor of English at Sul Ross State University and is presently on leave and working on a Ph.D. in folklore at The University of Texas.

LEON HALE, who travels much and writes feature columns for *The Houston Post* and books, is East Texas' favorite journalist.

FREDA HARDIN, NORBERT KORZENIEWSKI, TOMMY HOOP-ER, and DAVID HAMMERS are journalists, folklorists, and senior students in Gary High School.

JIM HARRIS is professor of English at New Mexico Junior College and fiction and folklore editor of *Southwest Heritage*.

WILSON M. HUDSON is a Fellow of the Texas Folklore Society, past Secretary-Editor, and professor emeritus of The University of Texas.

EUGENE MARTIN is a retired Nacogdoches County farmer who has the only syrup mill in town.

ARCHIE MCDONALD is a professor of history at Stephen F. Austin State University and editor of the *East Texas Historical Journal*.

CECIL OVERSTREET is a native of the Big Thicket and is the Justice of the Peace in Kountze.

RALPH RAMOS (deceased April, 1975) was a TV personality, photographer, journalist and a writer for the *Beaumont Enterprise*, whose specialty was the collection of East Texas folklore.

TIM SCHEER is a professional photographer, presently associated with Veeder Photography in Dallas.

ERNEST B. SPECK is a professor of English at Sul Ross State University.

KIT VAN CLEAVE is a professional writer and photographer working in Houston.

TIM VAN RIPER is a free-lance photo-journalist living in Nacogdoches.

C. W. WIMBERLEY of Wimberley is a native of the central Texas cedar brakes and is presently a columnist for the *Wimberley Mill*.

TFS HISTORY

History

The Texas Folklore Society was founded jointly by John Avery Lomax and Leonidas Warren Payne, Jr. When Lomax returned in 1907 from his year at Harvard he brought with him George Lyman Kittredge's suggestion that he establish an organization for collecting Texas folklore. Payne, who had come to The University of Texas in 1906 to teach English, was interested in folk speech. Conversations between Payne and Lomax, then teaching at Texas A&M, led to the presentation at the 1909 meeting of the Texas State Teachers Association in Dallas of a resolution to form "The Folk-Lore Society of Texas." Payne became the first president and Lomax the first secretary, and together they worked out plans and details. By April 10 they had enrolled ninety-two charter members.

Next to the American Folklore Society, the Texas Folklore Society is the oldest folklore organization still functioning in the United States. The first meeting was held on the campus of The University of Texas in 1911. Mrs. Bess Brown Lomax was on the program with a paper on the now famous "Boll Weevil" song, which Lomax had collected in the Brazos bottom in 1909. (He had returned to The University in 1910.) Kittredge attended the third meeting and gave three talks. Annual meetings have continued regularly since 1911, except for interruptions in 1918-1921 and 1944-45 caused by the great wars of their aftereffects. The Society has stimulated the recording and study of the rich folk culture of Texas and the Southwest, has attracted both laymen and scholars, and has distributed its publications throughout America and the world.

Annual Meetings

The Society meets just before Easter, when members read papers on a variety of folklore subjects. On Thursday night there is a "sing" and on Friday night a dinner with an invited speaker. All sessions are open to the public. Occasionally the Society combines a meeting and an outing, as when it met in Alpine and visited the Big Bend.

Publications

In 1916 Stith Thompson, then secretary, oversaw the publication of the Society's first volume, for which Kittredge wrote the preface. This volume was entitled Publication No. I, and was reprinted in 1935 as *Round the Levee*. In 1923 J. Frank Dobie took over as secretary-treasurer, and in the following twenty years of his tenure edited an impressive collection of Texas and Mexican border lore in sixteen numbered volumes. Ever since Publication No. II was issued in 1923, the Society has sent out a book annually to its members, although some have not been numbered publications of its own.

The tradition established by J. Frank Dobie was continued by Mody C. Boatright when he assumed the office of secretary-editor in 1943. He had assisted Dobie in editing Dobie's last five volumes. Harry Ransom also participated in editing the last four. Boatright served for twenty years and produced fifteen volumes. He was succeeded by Wilson M. Hudson, who had been associate editor since 1951. In 1971 the Society's office was moved to the Stephen F. Austin State University campus in Nacogdoches, and Francis Edward Abernethy became the secretary-editor.

The volumes published by the Society contain many of the papers read at its meetings and other articles both volunteered and solicited. Most contributions are the product of original collection, and together they constitute a wealth of material in the various branches of folklore. Some topics dealt with in past publications are home remedies for man and beast, cowboy songs, Negro songs and tales, games, oil field lore, diction used in various occupations, tales of the border Mexicans, German customs, superstitions, weather signs, yarns about birds and snakes, Indian myths and legends, the origins of place names, lore of the high plains, of the Gulf coast, of the brush country, household rhymes, and traditional songs. *Texas Folk and Folklore* (1954) is made up of items that appeared in earlier volumes. In recent publications the amount of space devoted to folklore studies as distinguished from folklore collections has increased.

Membership

Although the Society was originated by college teachers and has always had its office on a university campus, it is not exclusively academic in its membership. Its members are doctors, lawyers, bankers, ranchers, farmers, businessmen, and housewives. Anyone may join, whether a resident of Texas or not. Libraries and other institutions belong to the Society and have continuation subscriptions to our publications.

Membership is recorded upon payment of the annual dues of $7.50, and members receive the annual publication or some other folklore book selected by the editors for distribution in the years when a book is not brought out by the Society.

This is a nonprofit organization; money received from dues pays the cost of printing or purchasing the annual volume. The small margin left over from the sale of books to nonmembers is applied to the expenses of the office.

Our emblem is the roadrunner, called *paisano* by border folk, which epitomizes the free spirit of the brush country. J. Frank Dobie chose the paisano for the Society—and for himself—years ago.

Manuscripts

Unsolicited manuscripts and art work are accepted from members only, and they cannot be returned unless they are accompanied by a self-addressed, stamped envelope. The editor will take every precaution to prevent loss of manuscripts, but no responsibility can be assumed for unsolicited materials.

Address communications to:

The Texas Folklore Society
University Station
Nacogdoches, Texas 75961

INDEX

151

SOME STILL DO: ESSAYS ON TEXAS CUSTOMS   153

Type set by G & S TYPESETTERS
Printed by CAPITOL PRINTING COMPANY
Paper supplied by LONE STAR PAPER COMPANY
Bound by CUSTOM BOOKBINDERS
Design by WILLIAM D. WITTLIFF